Little Book of Big Emotions

Little Book of
Big Emotions

*How Five Feelings Affect Everything You Do
(and Don't Do)*

Erika M. Hunter

■ HAZELDEN®

Hazelden
Center City, Minnesota 55012-0176

1-800-328-0094
1-651-213-4590 (Fax)
www.hazelden.org

Library of Congress Cataloging-in-Publication Data

Hunter, Erika M., 1952–
    Little book of big emotions : how five feelings affect everything
    you do (and don't do) / Erika M. Hunter.
        p.   cm.
    Includes bibliographical references and index.
    ISBN 1-59285-079-0 (softcover)
    1. Emotions.   I. Title.
    BF531.H787 2004
    152.4—dc22

                                                      2004052380

08 07 06 05 04 6 5 4 3 2 1

Cover design by David Spohn
Interior design by Rachel Holscher
Typesetting by Stanton Publication Services, Inc.

Editor's note
The personal stories in this book are drawn from the author's life and work experiences. Names and situations have been changed to protect confidentiality. In some cases, composites have been created.

This book is not intended as a substitute for the advice and treatment of mental health professionals. The reader should consult these professionals in matters relating to his or her health.

For John, my Angel Dear

Contents

Acknowledgments

As with any book, this one evolved from interacting with others. I especially want to thank my friends Larraine Boyd, Michele Swisher, and Candice Chase for your loving look at this book. Without your support, humor, and feedback, I would not have had as much fun. Thank you, friends and family, especially my brother Mark whose honesty, care, and love are a shimmering oasis. Thank you to all who have explicitly and implicitly stimulated my emotional development, including those with whom I have struggled.

Thank you, Molly Hyslop and Pat and Peter Phillips, for your constancy and your stunning, unabashed maturity. Thank you, Dr. Jeff Savitsky and Dr. Gerry Work, for your interest and your intellectual challenges, and Daniel Boylan for your genuine love of the English language as well as for your students.

Additionally, special thanks to a number of marvelous human beings and doctors: Lorri Smith, Gillian Martlew, Marilyn Svihovec, and Stephen Clark.

I also thank those authors whose hard times gave them wisdom they have so generously shared through their books, including Sharon Wegscheider-Cruse, Melody Beattie, Pia Mellody, and Alice Miller, among many others.

Thank you so much, Karen, for believing in the message! My

editor at Hazelden, Karen Chernyaev, has patiently, consistently, and cheerfully contributed her guiding hand to shaping the focus and flow of this book. Through your excellent questions, comments, and astute editing skills, you have known when to grab the wheel and bring the vehicle back onto the road with a smile. Thank you!

Thank you, Kate Kjorlien, also from Hazelden, for your amazing clarity and deft handling of wayward sentences. Many thanks for your splendid "catches"!

My dear and beautiful husband and friend, you keep my heart aloft and happy. Bless you for your substantive subtle intelligence and your steadfast integrity, humor, and deep love. Your skills as reader and editor are, as ever, invaluable. Beautiful beacon of human possibility, you bridge the worlds of dreams and *gravitas* and let me trundle along. Thank you.

And last and very important, thank you Nikki, Petunia, and Frankie for keeping watch with me.

INTRODUCTION

Wherein I Discover Feelings
My Own

I graduated in 1978 with a master's degree focused on community counseling. For me, the degree was merely confirmation of what I'd been doing all my life: listening to people and supporting them. The odd thing was that at age twenty-five, after having been fully trained in therapeutic matters, I was no more responsible for or understanding of my emotions than were most people.

There was something missing in my education, in the transition and translation from studying psychotherapeutic theory to incorporating useful techniques—not for dealing with clients, but for understanding myself.

EMOTIONAL INGREDIENTS: IT'S NOT CAKE

Soon after I received my degree in counseling, I decided to see a therapist for myself—not for course work. She asked me a question I could not answer: "How do you feel?"

"Upset," I said.

She said, "Upset is not a feeling. It is a euphemism for a feeling."

I then asked, "What do you mean? I am upset."

"Okay, if you insist, but what does upset mean to you?"

That's when I was baffled. I was being asked for the ingredients of the cake, and all I could say was "cake." I had neither the emotional vocabulary nor the ability to take the cake and identify its ingredients. No one had ever asked me this question before and been so picky about my response. No one had ever asked me what was underneath. I felt scared because, frankly, my other answer had always gotten me by. I felt humiliated too, that, after all my "learning," I was personally illiterate in the language of my trade.

I was given a short list of basic descriptors—mad, sad, glad, scared, and ashamed—and then was asked to take time throughout each day to check in with myself as to how I was feeling. This was not natural. I felt foolish, initially, and had to take on faith my therapist's word that checking in with how I was feeling would somehow be a good thing. I considered it to be a grueling yet exciting task. Grueling because I was unskilled. Exciting because every time I matched the appropriate feeling name with the emotion, there was a release and a rightness about having done so. I felt a "cleanness" and delight in knowing something about myself that was honest, unique, and my own. Whether the energy transforms, dissipates, evaporates, or shifts, I don't know. But there is definitely a pronounced release and freedom in owning basic feelings.

I could not believe that I had lived a quarter of a century, gotten my degree, and was only just now learning how to feel, accept, and understand coursing emotional energy.

Growing up, I had been given some fairly narrow parameters in which to name my experiences. I had, through the institutions of family, education, religion, and culture, been brought up with a fairly comprehensive set of guidelines about how females are to "be." The first guideline was that children's spirits need to be caged in order to keep the children from getting out of control. The tighter the rules, the "better" the child. Another guideline was that females are not in the same class as men. They have their own special roles to fulfill, but those are not the roles of men. So, instead of *being*, I was *doing for*. Instead of living in my own life, I was living for others' lives. This mind-set kept me externally focused. But it began to change when my therapist's exercise brought me up short. I had to begin feeling *my* reactions and responses. And of course, I found this hard.

I began with "checking in." When I was at work, I would take a moment to ask myself, "How do I feel right now?" Because I was a beginner, I had to try each feeling on. I couldn't just say "I'm scared" because I didn't know how. I was not able to sort out the simplest of combined emotional ingredients without going through the process of comparing how I felt against each basic feeling. "Am I angry?" I would ask myself. If I were not, I would try on another feeling until I felt the thrill of recognition. Each ingredient seemed a defining moment, a partial answer to who I was.

As I grew more competent, I began to experience a singular joy and sense of personal power. It was like hitting a mini-jackpot each time, with the winnings accumulating in a private account.

From that point forward, no one could ever tell me, "Don't feel that way." No one and no institution could ever say, "That's not what you're feeling" with any kind of import, because I now knew with a deep certainty what I was feeling. My feelings became a given, unable to be changed for someone else's benefit or to suit another's mood.

And so I learned to identify, name, and take responsibility for my feelings, a process that will be detailed later in this book. This was the beginning of what continues to be incredible personal freedom. Feelings are as natural as breathing. Whether I choose to act on them, when I choose to act on them, where they come from, and why they arise are other parts of the puzzle, which will also be described later.

I learned that upset in one circumstance might be anger or it might be fear, or it might be combined with hurt and shame. I learned to say "I'm hurt" or "I'm angry," at first only to myself, and later to others. I was able to label situations that led to my feelings. I began seeing patterns of how I live in the world. Something that had previously been a cloudy and amorphous mass of upheaval—triggered and reacted to—became a manageable and understandable series of events.

I was free! I was free to experience the full range of my emotional repertoire, whether acceptable to others or not. My feelings are a direct connection to my heart, to immediacy and vulnerability, but they are also tempered by my thoughts about how to act in appropriate and responsible ways. Wow! As long as I do not act on every feeling I have, I can experience my emotions and learn from them. Plus, learning that I do not have to do anything about how I feel was a huge relief. I can feel scared, and instead of avoiding the situation that I feel fearful in, I can say that I feel afraid and go through the situation. I don't have to act scared, and I don't have to pretend I'm not afraid.

MOVING FORWARD

By learning to identify what I was feeling, by calling various emotions by their most basic names, I slowly began to see the world in a different way. Instead of either ignoring how I was affected by others or ignoring how I was affecting them, I began to become much more conscious and aware. I was able to see and stop patterns of behavior that were not beneficial. I acquired a solid vocabulary, which helped me take emotional responsibility, set limits, and own my part in misunderstandings. I learned to clear out my errors on a daily basis and make corrections, which eventually led to a clear, positive, and more mature role in the world, as well as in my personal relationships.

ONE

Emotions = Energy

Emotions, or feelings, equal energy—energy we can free up and use. By not acknowledging feelings, we are pretty much saying no to free electricity. Whether we like, use, or acknowledge emotions, they are part of the mystery of the human condition. This book helps us tap into the mysteries and benefits of becoming familiar with our emotions.

This book is simple. It is a tool kit. First, it describes the five basic emotions: anger, fear, gladness, sorrow, and shame. Second, it offers ways to identify *all* feelings, not just the ones we find easy to feel or express. Third, it explains the difference between *having* feelings and *acting* on them. And last, it presents a way to take responsibility for our feelings, so others won't have to.

What are the benefits to us? We'll be clearer about who we are and why. We will lose some of our fears about experiencing feelings because we will know what they are and what to do with them. We will find our own ways to release emotions before we become controlled by them. We may also find that we no longer need to overreact or act out when we feel certain emotions. We will understand what the force of those feelings is about, and we will know what to do when we feel that force.

THE GOAL OF THIS BOOK

The goal of this book is to help us free up energy so we can use our time and electricity for more constructive, important, and relevant projects. The energy I'm talking about is associated with those little feelings that crop up throughout the day. We may not even be aware of them, or we may consider them too unimportant to pay attention. But what if, instead of leaving the little feelings unexpressed and left to build up and perhaps explode, we choose to recognize and release them?

We can either flow with or resist the tremendous and constant stream of emotions that are part of being alive. It's a bigger matter than just saying "no" to feelings or unconsciously ignoring them. When we ignore our emotions, there are consequences for us, our friends and colleagues, and even our "enemies." And there are consequences for innocent bystanders, including children, for whom the secondhand emotions can be just as toxic as secondhand smoke.

If we're the *resisting type,* if we don't have an emotional vocabulary, or if we want only to be rational about emotions, then someone somewhere *will*—someone somewhere *must*—pay for our feelings, for the unexpended energy. And that someone is often not even directly involved with how we are feeling. We can learn to become aware of how we take our feelings out on others, whether a stranger or a child. We can learn how to use our emotions constructively so that we get more of what we want, and so that those who know us do as well.

If we are *not the resisting type,* we have an awareness of feelings. We may find it invigorating to acknowledge feelings and their messages to us. We may enjoy the clarity that comes by saying, "I feel angry because someone cut in front of me in traffic, *not* because my children are laughing loudly while I drive." By feeling the emotion, identifying it, and understanding its message, we release the energy associated with the emotion. We can talk to our kids without yelling. We don't go down the path of feeling angry about all the times we've been cut off, and we don't rant, "What is the world coming to?" The event, our emotional response to it, and the release of energy are over almost before they begin when we take responsibility for our emotions. It's that simple.

HAVING EMOTIONS VERSUS *BEING* EMOTIONAL

Because we are human, we have emotions. But just because we have emotions does not mean we are *emotional*. Even though it may feel like we *are* the anger when we say "I am angry," it isn't true. We have emotions, but we have them within the context of all the other things we are. We do not say "I am a husband," and that's the end of the story. The same is true with emotions. We only experience them.

It is healthy to have emotions, to experience them, to integrate the lessons we learn from them, to use them for guidance and clues about who we are, and to use them to garner information about the world. It is unnatural not to have feelings. But *having* feelings and *indulging* in them are two different things.

When we are denied, or deny ourselves, the freedom to feel, express verbally, and take responsibility for emotions, we create unspent emotional energy in ourselves. Holding back about the nature and truth of our feelings builds up. When all the emotion and its energy rush out at once, some of us become physically abusive or violent. Others become verbally abusive and blaming, twisting the energy into hurtful words. These kinds of responses neither resolve the problem nor release the energy.

Notice the difference between *expressing* emotions and *acting* on them. To express an emotion, we use words. We say things such as "I feel angry" or "I feel hurt." To act on an emotion, we do something to get rid of the energy that goes with the feeling. Either we can *act on* a feeling or we can *act out*. Acting on an emotion implies that we cry, take a long walk, talk with someone, or make changes in our attitudes or our lives. We release the energy of our emotions without harming or transferring the energy on to others. But many of us think that expressing emotions and/or acting on them is the same as acting out emotions. When we act out, we may hit, scream, or use abusive language toward others and rationalize our behavior by saying it is how we feel.

We are not our emotions. We experience them—they are a part of us. We are responsible for acknowledging our emotions, but emotions are not excuses for abusive language or hurtful actions toward others. We are responsible for releasing the energy associated with emotions in healthy ways. There are many ways to do this, but to begin with, we need to name our emotions. This is the starting point. We will learn about how to do this throughout the book.

EXERCISING EMOTIONS

We can liken our emotions to our muscles. Everyone has muscles, but not everyone becomes a bodybuilder. Even if we aren't bodybuilders, we know we have the capacity to build muscles and we use our muscles throughout the day without consciously thinking about them. We also know that if we were to lie in bed for several months, the muscles would become stiffened and atrophied. We would have to be patient in remembering how to walk again. We would not just hop out of bed feeling strong and capable. We would have to begin an exercise program and gradually strengthen and rebuild the muscles until they could bear our weight again.

We also use our emotions without consciously thinking about them. Our emotions are part of the infrastructure that courses through our daily lives. We become more aware of our feelings when they get a lot of "exercise," as in when we become very sad, angry, or frightened. But for the most part, many of us don't give our everyday emotions a whole lot of attention.

Being able to identify and understand the five basic feelings lets us take more control of our feelings, not less. When it comes to emotions, ignorance is not bliss. Knowing gives us the power to control our feelings, instead of having them control our behavior or make us feel as if we're losing our mind. We can't escape from our feelings—not without consequences. But by learning to listen to and work with our feelings, we can be more in control of our lives, rather than feeling compelled, impelled, propelled, expelled, or repelled by our emotions.

Taxes and death are certainties. So are feelings, and sometimes they are about as welcome! But if we consider our feelings as helpful energy, valuable sources of information, and messengers meant to keep us informed, we begin bringing their energy under our control. This practice exercises our emotional muscles.

The Source of Jack's Important Decision

Jack became a trial lawyer and spent his days arguing for his clients' sake. He was well into his career when he began getting counseling. By working through his emotions, Jack realized he didn't really like arguing. He had spent years in college in order to win the arguments in the courtroom that he could not win at home with his domineering alcoholic father.

Jack's example demonstrates the value of listening to emotions as sources of information.

HOLDING BACK

Each of us finds certain emotions easier to experience and express than others. By not acknowledging or expressing the feelings that are more difficult for us, we may be cutting off our ability to experience the range of all our emotions. For example, Jason dislikes intensely what he regards as the *weaker* emotions, meaning fear and sorrow. His tendency is to get angry rather than cry. He makes judgments about men who cry. When his girlfriend's dog died, Jason felt no need to comfort her because he has no relationship with sorrow and the release that comes from crying. His perceived lack of support caused his girlfriend to break up with him. This made him angry. At what point will Jason understand or experience loss? What will it take for him to see his resistance as a liability?

When we pick and choose which emotions we are willing to feel, we may lose access to important clues about ourselves. For example, Jeremy works hard all day. When he gets home, his wife says, "Now it's your turn to take care of the kids while I take a break." As a result, the only time Jeremy has for himself is late at night when he is too exhausted to think. Jeremy's wife does not know he wants or needs time for himself. He doesn't tell her because he is invested in being a "good" husband, which doesn't include being angry or wanting things for himself. Jeremy gets his good feelings from, in his words, "being a good provider." Being a good provider doesn't include being a "taker." Avoiding his needs includes avoiding his anger and avoiding the acknowledgment of his wants. Over time, Jeremy's love for his life lessens as he just goes through the motions.

By failing to name reactions accurately, we inadvertently hold on to energy associated with feelings and events. Over time, unexpressed emotions become unresolved issues, which create stress and have health-related ramifications.

DECIDING TO EXPAND OUR RANGE

If we learn *how* to feel the range of emotions and the energy that comes with them, we can be in charge of our responses. We learn more about ourselves. As a result, we are better able to live life as fearless and whole people. We have an ever-expanding capacity for gladness, as well as a larger capacity for sorrow, fear, shame, and anger. Others will begin to know us, and we will no longer live in isolation and loneliness.

Some of us don't know what we're missing. We don't have access to our emotions, and we can't imagine what they feel like or what good could come of them. The difference between these worlds can be as big as the difference between what a child at four knows and what a child at seventeen understands, or the difference between dating and falling in love. We can't know until we get there. Think of two turtles—one from a pond and one from an ocean—sharing stories. The pond turtle cannot comprehend the magnificence of the ocean because his pond environment is limited. The ocean turtle invites the pond turtle to go with him to the ocean because he knows that the pond turtle will only truly understand by seeing for himself.

It's never too late to redress our development or let our emotions contribute to our lives. Whenever we begin, we will slowly grow into another realm so rich and meaningful that we can't believe we didn't know it existed. And we will want more.

SOCIAL AND CULTURAL VALUES ABOUT EMOTIONS

The most basic spiritual, emotional, and intellectual questions about life and our purpose often get posed during adolescence. The questions arise from the sudden realization that we are "someone." This developmental stage asks the big questions:

Who am I? Why am I here? How should I live my life, and for what purpose? The only way to satisfy these questions is through the interplay of our physical, spiritual, emotional, and mental being. We are a combination of the following—and many more— characteristics:

- Biological: We are physical bodies with specific apti-
  tudes, weaknesses, chemistry, and appearances.
- Sexual: We are male, female, or on a continuum of
  sexuality with a combination of qualities.
- Spiritual: We each have beliefs, whether or not we fol-
  low an organized religion.
- Mental: We think, figure things out, and create.
- Emotional: We have feelings, and we choose whether
  or not to act on them.
- Social: We interact with others or choose not to interact.

How do we find answers to these important questions that will satisfy us and be congruent with our deepest understandings? It is a lifelong process, but we have help. Most of our physical, mental, and spiritual wants and needs are universally acknowledged. Help and assistance are found through medicine, education, community resources, media, and religious groups, to name a few. Sometimes the help is not a good match for our need, but at least, as a society, we attempt to provide recognition and assistance.

We are not, however, as overt or proactive when it comes to emotional wellness. In all likelihood, most of us did not have someone sit with us and ask us about our feelings as we were growing up. We probably did not have five basic feelings identified for us, and we were probably not given ways to name our experiences. Imagine how life might have been had our emotional experiences been valued by classmates, teachers, parents, siblings, religious leaders, friends, lovers, colleagues, and institutions.

But talking about emotions is not quite as welcome or accepted as talking about health problems. Often, when we see a therapist, we may not want anyone to know about it. An unspoken stigma is associated with needing help with our emotions. We go to therapists to get "our head shrunk." We see the "head" doctor and are labeled "mental patients." We call the whole messy emotional thing another name—psychology, psychiatry, psychotherapy—instead of emotional assistance. Why the intrigue?

We have few systems that guide, educate, and support our emotional wellness. Why is that? We are taught the five primary colors, but not the five primary feelings. Many kids are already bundles of pent-up emotional histories by the time they learn their colors. We are taught about character and morality; we are taught public speaking and communication skills; but we are not, as a matter of course, taught the names of feelings, how to recognize them, or what to do with them when we have them.

How can we answer the question "Who am I?" if we don't have the words? How can we avoid destructively acting out if we do not have the vocabulary for discussing emotional issues? What if we could learn early on to express our emotions, value them, and take responsibility for them?

LISTENING AND LEARNING

To know what *someone else* is feeling, we listen. To know what *we* are feeling, we listen. Listening to others includes looking directly at the person speaking, holding back our experiences and judgments, and acknowledging to ourselves that we do not know how this other person is feeling. To be an effective listener, our attitude is important. We must be humble and let go of the need to be right, the need to control, and even the need to pay back someone else for previous wrongs. We must hold back our own need to be listened to and give our full attention to the other person. This is not easy. As we listen, we may have many thoughts and feelings ourselves, but we can share them when it is our turn to be listened to. (This will be addressed in more detail in chapter 9, "Communication Skills.")

We must also actively listen to ourselves, regularly giving our emotions our full attention. Emotions are internal messengers. If we do not learn how to listen to our feelings, we accumulate more unexpressed energy. This creates patterns of avoidance or acting out that are then passed on to others. For example, if we don't try to understand the language of feelings in our children, we may unintentionally set them up to *act out* what they are feeling. Instead of teaching them how to talk to us by using terms that describe emotions, we may unintentionally silence them.

If we don't teach children emotional responsibility, we teach them to become adults in age only. If children pass into adulthood without having learned emotional responsibility, they may find it easy to lie, cheat, or hurt others because emotions are not part of their consciousness. They may learn to avoid feeling, to take the easy way out, and to stop striving to be authentic. Sometimes it is not what someone does but what someone fails to do that affects others. And not teaching emotional responsibility can lead to anything from rudeness to acts of violence.

When parents learn to be emotionally responsible, they teach through example. Children then have the tools to make informed choices. Their "mistakes" become ways of learning.

Susan's Emotional Gaps

Many of us live our lives without using the important information that comes from emotions. For example, Susan is comfortable with being uncomfortable. She sees the world through the eyes of her powerlessness as a child, which now translates into feeling stepped on by colleagues who cannot and do not read her mind. When a colleague in the next cubicle talks loudly, Susan takes his insensitivity personally. She complains to her boss that this colleague has it in for her, and she begins stacking up perceived wrongs. Eventually, Susan adds to her powerlessness by seeing this person's actions as toward her, when, really, the colleague is simply unaware and insensitive. He is not intentionally attempting to ruin Susan's day.

Susan could learn from this situation. Instead of telling herself that her colleague has it in for her, Susan could (1) talk with him about what she needs, wants, and expects, (2) check out what about this situation feels familiar and why, (3) make a promise that for one week she won't blame anyone else for her feelings and reactions, and then see where this new attitude takes her, or (4) identify the feelings and beliefs she has about the larger issue of blame.

NO SUBSTITUTES

We cannot buy off our feelings, make substitutions, or shape our emotions into what is popular and acceptable to others without consequence. People in recovery from an addiction tell vivid stories about where their chemical substitutions have taken them. Emotional substitutions include drugs, money, power, food, relationships, gambling, and sex. We may turn to substitutes to fill up an empty place inside, to feel better and stave off bad feelings.

If we do not know how to read the messages of our emotions and if we do not have the language or tools to put our emotions to use, we turn to whatever makes us feel better—sometimes to excess, which leads to addiction. How is it, then, that so many people, at some point, are able to move forward in their lives and recover from their addictions? Support groups and rehabilitation programs give people the *emotional tools* to recover their lives. People learn how to listen and be listened to. They learn that the lessons of emotions can be experienced through support and guidance. They learn the freedom that comes from taking responsibility for their choices.

To lead healthy, whole lives, we experience our feelings, name them, and choose whether to act on them. No one else can do this for us. Our emotional lives are constantly changing, and our emotions are important clues to discovering what we truly value and who we will become. When we learn the language of emotions, we are freer to face life head-on.

MOVING FORWARD

We now know that emotions are more than words. They are energetic messengers that teach us about who we are. And when we release their energy in healthy ways, we gain important information that leads to understanding and maturity.

Next, we discover the basic emotions and what purpose each serves.

TWO

The Basic Emotions
What Are They?

There are five basic emotions: anger, fear, gladness, sorrow, and shame. These feelings may also be identified by other names, but we're going to keep to basics here and throughout the book. This chapter provides an overview of the basics with brief descriptions and examples of each feeling. (Subsequent chapters provide in-depth information about each of the five feelings, stories about people and emotions, and practical tools for mining our feelings, expressing them, and releasing them.)

It's helpful to think of feelings as being on a continuum. They may be big or small. They may be new or old. They may be justified or not.

A continuum appears at the beginning of each chapter detailing an emotion. Along each continuum are words describing the intensities and variations of the basic emotion. These expressions of each emotion are only partially accurate. They point to a deeper fundamental truth. By acknowledging the *core* emotion at the heart of each continuum, we find the key to releasing blocked energy.

When we begin to identify our core feelings, we can give even small feelings and old feelings room to be felt and then released. Each feeling has a story. The stories help us understand our emotions and ourselves, but we need to acquire the emotional language before we can tell the stories.

As humans, we are made to respond to our world. Our emotions ask us to respond. They tell us to get angry, feel sad, jump for joy, or do something because we're scared. When we dismiss the feelings, we dismiss the message. When we fail to respond to the message, the energy and issues don't just disappear. The energy remains an active force in our lives, as we can see when someone "blows his stack."

When we use a specific word to name the basic emotion, the energy dissipates. When we name our most basic emotions, we tell our story first to ourselves. We don't fool ourselves into thinking, for example, that we "never get angry." Just because we use words such as *frustrated, annoyed,* or *upset* doesn't mean that we never get angry. These are variations on the theme that can let us off the hook from knowing who we are. But by naming the basic emotions, we cut to the chase. For example, when we want to know that someone loves us, we may enjoy hearing that we are liked, cherished, valued, or cared for. But when someone says "I love you," we know what is meant.

ANGER

We'll discuss anger first, not because it is easy to deal with but because it is easy to identify. The energy of anger pushes us to do something. It is a powerful feeling. Anger may cause an outward reaction or an inward reaction. If we react outwardly, we may give someone the finger or swear. If we react inwardly, we may get mad at ourselves or put ourselves in a dangerous situation.

Is one way of reacting better than the other? There are consequences either way. Regardless, anger provides clues as to what our boundaries are or what needs to change in our relationships.

For example, three people are having lunch. One person insists on telling dirty stories. One listener enjoys this and laughs. The other person feels disgusted and gets angry. Laughter invites more stories, while anger puts up a barrier. Even if the second listener doesn't act on his feelings, his opinion of dirty stories will lead to a decision about whether to have lunch with these people again. Anger gives clues as to who we are, what we value, and how we prefer to live.

Many times, the stronger the feeling, the more important the clue.

The man who was offended has several options for addressing his feeling: He could say something now or later to either or both of his luncheon pals. He could privately ask the joker to refrain. He could say nothing. Voicing feelings works, not because the person won't tell jokes again but because our emotions related to the event are visible and released. It can also be a good idea to check the other person's reasons. For example, the man might say, "I am curious about why you are continuing to tell dirty stories after I asked you not to. Would you please explain?" This opens the line of communication, which is risky but also freeing.

SORROW

Sorrow is another powerful and telling basic emotion. Sorrow is the feeling that occurs when we lose something. We can lose people, objects, ideas, or opportunities. Our losses may be small or big, concrete or abstract. The feelings involved can be huge or negligible, and they can be from long ago or from today. Dealing with feelings of sorrow is often difficult. Feeling sad implies being vulnerable, and because sorrow is such a personal experience, it causes loneliness.

Sorrow, like the other basic emotions, has a tendency to build up. For example, if our beloved pet was killed by a car and we do not cry, the next time we have a loss, we will probably have two griefs to deal with.

When life deals us multiple losses, we create unnecessary burdens for ourselves if we continue to postpone the tears and the acknowledgment of pain. Over time, we may find it more and more difficult to cry about anything. Or we may suddenly cry for reasons totally unrelated to our pain, as when a television commercial sets us off. Or we may even cry in inappropriate places, as when we burst into tears in a meeting at work. We may be storing up such a flood of emotions that we become afraid to feel, especially when we are feeling more vulnerable with a new loss. We may begin to avoid topics that might make us cry. Others may avoid us, frightened by the urgency of our tears when we do express our sadness. Sorrow is not one of the more popular feelings because we must be willing to allow it to overtake us.

SHAME

Shame is experienced in a variety of emotional contexts. While shame may be made up of some of the other emotions, it is experienced as a single feeling. Shame differs from guilt. For the purposes of this book, *shame* is feeling bad about something that is not our fault. *Guilt*, on the other hand, is feeling bad about something that is our fault. We experience guilt because our actions or failure to act caused harm to others or ourselves. Shame, however, is typically put on us through the conscious or unconscious manipulation of others.

For example, a child is playing outside when the father comes home. The father tells the child, "Stop playing. Don't you know your mother is tired and needs help?" The child may feel shame because she didn't know her mother needed help. Often shame combines anger and fear. The anger may come from being expected to read someone's mind. The fear may come from not knowing how to "do it right" and the craving for love or positive attention that has been withdrawn. When we feel ashamed, we have a tendency to try to correct things that are not our fault or responsibility and that have no "right" answer. Being unable to "do it right" leaves us with attempts that end in failure. Thus, shame can be recognized by its no-win nature and the energy of helplessness. When guilty, one can say, "I did it. I'm sorry. I'll do my best not to do it again." But shame has no way out. Shame just settles in and creates discomfort, feelings of inadequacy, and hyperawareness for those burdened with another's blame.

FEAR

Fear is often easy to notice, at least on the surface. We feel fear and our hands get clammy, our heart pounds, our thoughts race, and we are short of breath. Fear certainly has an energy. We can run and hide, fight, or negotiate. Fear puts us in touch with our need for safety. When safety—whether emotional, financial, spiritual, or physical—is secured, it becomes part of our lives. We may take it for granted. Whether that safety comes from being valued in childhood, in our jobs, or through physical prowess, we unfold within it. We can even use this foundation of safety as a springboard to unfold in the larger world—as in when we venture outside the vision our parents have of us.

When warning sirens go off implying that our safety is threatened, the resulting adrenaline pushes us to act. Intense fear seems to skip thought and jump to impulse, which directs us to do whatever we must to protect ourselves. Survival fears, as instinctive as they are, may or may not be realistic. As we identify fears, we may bring them under our control. We can choose those fears we want to act on and those we want simply to acknowledge.

For example, when our heart races during a job interview, we don't need to run out of the room. We can acknowledge that we are scared, that we are vulnerable to the opinion of the person interviewing us, and just sit there with a smile and do what we need to do. But when our physical safety is threatened, fear gives us a strong signal that says we need to protect ourselves. We must act on these signals. For example, when we fear that another person may harm us, either from experience or intuition, we don't hang around to ask questions. We get away, go to a safe place, or ask for help immediately.

GLADNESS

Gladness is the easiest emotion to experience for most people. It is a delight that wells up and out of us—an energy that expresses a deep gratitude and keeps us in the moment. We can't force gladness, but we can certainly create situations in which it may result. Enjoy means "to take joy within." We'll look at how the energy of gladness can propel us to action and at how we can accept the ebb and flow of this emotion's often fleeting nature.

Why talk about feelings of gladness? Even with all the available "toys" that are meant to bring gladness, we seem to have a shortage of it in the busyness of the typical workweek. Gladness seems to spring from a kind of clarity and meets the needs of the heart—a contented heart—instead of the head or ego. And at its most potent, being glad is the umbrella under which many aspects of the good life may be found.

Pleasure is a type of physical happiness that comes from our senses. We see, smell, hear, taste, and touch life in ways that give us pleasure. The source comes from outside us. Contentment and joy, on the other hand, are interior understandings of our place in the world, where spiritual, emotional, and creative meaningfulness come unbidden. It is an unforced fulfillment that is hard to duplicate.

For example, I was recently at an outdoor concert. I saw mothers and fathers dancing with their babies in the early evening light. They seemed to be in the moment. I saw no gadgets. I heard no cell phones. I saw no toys. Music, warmth, freedom to move about, and the faces of children seemed to meet the requirements for contentment and even joy. And that energy was contagious.

WHAT ELSE WILL I FIND IN THIS BOOK?

You'll find more about each of the five basic feelings in the following chapters. You'll also find some information about closely related topics. For example, you can read about communication skills: what each of us needs in order to share our emotional perspectives with others.

Feel free to skip around in the book as needed.

The next chapter discusses where feelings, as energy, go. You'll find the individual feelings discussed in depth, starting with anger in chapter 4.

THREE

Where Do Feelings Go?
Emotional Energy

When I was young, I was malleable and agreeable. I thought I could hide all the feelings I didn't like. I put ideas and feelings that I believed would make me a bad person in a safe place—at the back of my make-believe closet—and slammed the door shut. Initially, the closet didn't look crowded or full; however, this space was neither limitless nor harmless. Eventually, the emotions found their way out and ended up in my life. They intruded at will, it seemed, until I found ways to release them and learn from them.

As a young adult, I made some mistakes over and over. Arguments seemed to revolve around the same issues. Instead of gaining insight and moving on, I followed the same patterns over and over again. The strength of my feelings grew: more arguing with less satisfaction. One day, I realized that *something* was beginning to build up in my closet. I didn't know how to clean it out or lessen the amount of stuff in there. I was having a hard time closing that door. My previous composure was developing some stress fractures.

Needless to say, I didn't like the idea that emotions could not be stuffed indefinitely. I had been taught that it was wrong to express certain emotions and that to do so could hurt others. Because all these emotional discards still belonged to me, I was the only one who could come to grips and figure out what to do with them. This meant I had to change. I had to learn new ways to deal with my emotional life. I began to sense a tremendous amount of energy involved—a powerhouse of possibilities lying around longing to be unleashed.

EMOTIONS WANT A PLACE TO GO

Now that I have worked through many exercises in emotional problem solving, I understand that when I toss a feeling back into that closet, I toss back energy. Emotions are made of energy that can cause us to feel restless, burdened, or uncomfortable. When we try to act as though emotions are static, dead, or mere words that mean nothing, they intrude into our lives. We are amazed when, seemingly out of nowhere, we do something surprising and even embarrassing: so-called Freudian slips.

In the movie *Roxanne*, based loosely on the story of Cyrano de Bergerac, the new fireman, when introduced to the chief, is given explicit instructions not to look at or comment on the outrageous size of the chief's nose. The fireman can't help himself. He says something like "I am happy to meet your nose." He can't take his eyes or his mind from it. If the fireman had had no emotional reaction, he would have been able to be courteous, but the energy of his emotion compelled him to say words he was trying hard to suppress.

When we comment or do something out of character, we may say, "I don't know why, but all of a sudden I couldn't help it." Knowing emotional language helps us translate a feeling into an idea, whether we express the energy in the moment or at a later time. If we accept that emotions have energy, we can control them better. We have a kind of army of emotions at our disposal to be used as needed, but if we don't get to know our "troops," we may find treason and mutiny when we're ready to do battle.

That is not to say we should express every emotion. Common sense says we can save emotions to use for our own purposes. We may want to keep some of our anger available for a competition we're involved in. We may use fear to motivate us toward refining a technique, as in practicing skiing. We may save sadness for a time when we have no other commitments or for when we are in the comfort of a friend's home. We can choose when and how to release and use our emotions.

However, when we hold back out of fear, when there is no plan, when feelings depress, paralyze, compel us to negative actions, or keep us from evolving, then we are not making conscious choices about them. Habitually holding back or acting out emotions keeps us in patterns. And when patterns of hair-trigger tempers, unsuccessful relationships with people, terrible loneliness, suicidal thinking, or homicidal rages drive us, we are being given a big clue. It is time to learn how to notice, name, and choose how to use emotional energy.

SO, WHAT DO WE DO WITH FEELINGS?

In the throes of emotion, we have three choices. Many of our responses are not conscious; we simply react. Having choices let's us change our reactions. Being aware of our options is the first step.

Emotional Choices	Consequences
Hold the emotions inside.	Creates a dangerous possibility that we will be emotionally invisible to friends, relatives, colleagues, strangers, and children, as well as to ourselves. If we do not allow others to know us, how will our lives be reflected back to us? *Social invisibility* can lead to devastating loneliness and meaninglessness.

Release the emotions on others.	Creates a dangerous possibility of alienating others or harming them verbally or physically. Squelches love. The outside action belies the pain and suffering inside. Again, we end up being unknown and may spread our misery to others.
Note the emotions by calling them the appropriate name, feeling them, choosing whom to talk to about them, and choosing whether to act on them.	Creates self-confidence, self-control, and emotional health that releases the energy of the emotions and teaches us about the world and ourselves. We are visible to others and ourselves and, thus, we become known. Love can then flourish in the truth, respect, openness, and vulnerability.

Once we gain some awareness of our reactions, we can take a term such as *jealousy* and pull it apart so that we can see why we feel jealous. In this example, Marcy is jealous of an acquaintance, Annie, who has been elected to the school board. Marcy has never run for the board, but she feels jealous anyway. The following chart pulls out some of the emotional ingredients of jealousy.

Complex Feeling	Ingredients
Jealousy	**Anger:** Marcy compares herself with Annie and feels she doesn't measure up. **Anger:** Marcy is angry with herself for failing to take a risk, do the legwork, and attain what Annie has.

	Anger: Marcy is angry with those who she thinks are blocking her goals, including the Divine, parents, family, and so on.
	Fear: Marcy is afraid she will never be able to do what Annie is doing.
	Shame: Marcy feels ashamed because she thinks she cannot succeed.

If Marcy takes time to see what lies behind her jealousy, she will see that she wants to become active in her community, whether by joining the school board or in some other capacity. She wants a voice and has her ideas. However, she has not done any of the legwork. Jealousy can be an excellent road map that points in directions hidden by our excuses. We can take action, lose the victimization and jealousy, and succeed in realizing important dreams! The energy of jealousy's ingredients can propel Marcy to attain her goals.

WHAT HAPPENS WHEN WE IGNORE OUR EMOTIONS?

If we have learned that it is impolite, inappropriate, or shameful to have emotional issues or that they are signs of failure, it will be harder to let others and ourselves know the truth. Emotional struggles are normal. To admit we are "having a problem" with a co-worker, our finances, or a child is not cause for describing ourselves as failures. These kinds of situations are part of the many opportunities we have as humans to evolve, to learn life's lessons, and to have something real to share with others.

When we have an "I've got it all together" attitude, even

with our closest friends, spouse, or parents, then we will feel alone—alone in the sense of never being known. Perfection carries with it invulnerability, and both are hard for most of us to identify with. So when we let others know we are imperfect, they understand us and subsequently love us. We feel closer to others when we share our humanity, both the struggles and successes. If we don't let anyone in, we remain invisible; others can only guess at what is going on with us. We unintentionally create superficial relationships that support only our facade, which often reinforces our unexplored doubts.

We have many ways to avoid our feelings. We can substitute behaviors that sidetrack us from taking emotional responsibility. For example, we may find it easier to love a child than a spouse; easier to kick the dog than to confront the boss; or easier to give another driver "the finger" than to admit we were driving too fast. It may seem at the time that we have outwitted the emotional energy, but these are not benign releases. No one is getting away with anything. Ultimately, those who end up paying our emotional debts avoid us, and our unclaimed emotional energy just keeps cycling around to get our attention.

Despite the many paths of emotional avoidance, many of us do choose to listen to what our emotions have to say. But what if we are mistaken in how we interpret our feelings?

WHAT HAPPENS WHEN WE
MISINTERPRET STRONG EMOTIONS?

There is no doubt about it: As we go through the business of learning about others and ourselves, we are bound to make mistakes. Lots of them, in fact. And when we do, it can be cause for gratitude, because it means we have taken a risk and may learn something that could eventually become wisdom. However, when we have strong emotional reactions, we tend to think they are justified (meaning that we have a *right* to act on them). Sometimes we act without thinking about the possibility that our reaction is not justified. We don't bother with looking at the other side. When we "know" we're right, we tend to feed the fires of our imagination.

The truth about how our reaction connects to an emotion may not be that simple. Having an emotion does not justify acting on it. Feeling an emotion does not mean that someone else is to blame. We may have old issues related to the current situation that influence our interpretation. When we have strong emotions, there are some simple safeguards to observe.

We can check to see whether we're being triggered, whether we are making assumptions, and whether we are justifying or blaming. By reviewing these possibilities, we can better choose how to release and act on our emotions.

Checking Out Our Perceptions	
Getting Triggered	Reacting to a current situation with the strength of unresolved emotions connected to earlier emotional wounds.
Making Assumptions	Guessing at what's behind someone else's motives, actions, words, and thoughts. The guess typically either supports a belief system we are invested in or gives us permission to act out.
Justifying or Blaming	Telling ourselves that we have every right to act out on someone else because he or she has made us feel a certain way. Ideas of fairness, deserving, justice, or revenge crop up.

Getting Triggered: Jim's Story

Jim grew up with parents who "knew better." Jim wanted to work as an artist in graphic design, but Jim's father insisted he attend a business college. Jim graduated with a degree in economics and got a job as a retail manager. Sometimes he made suggestions to the owner of the business about what products seemed to be selling best with certain customers.

Jim began thinking his boss was ignoring his ideas. The anger he felt about "not being important" was deep and intense. Even Jim was surprised at the force of his reaction. When Jim finally sat down and talked with his boss, his boss told him that orders were based on statistical information. Once Jim heard his boss's take, he realized that his boss actually had a good track record when it came to listening to all the employees.

Jim reviewed his own behavior and was amazed at how he had significantly misconstrued his boss's motives. Jim realized that his reaction to his boss was really attached to earlier experiences with his father. Jim's overreaction, a look at the boss's track record, and a bit of detective work involving why being ignored felt familiar helped Jim understand and let go of this issue. Jim was now freed from expecting his boss to make up for his father's lack of parenting skills.

Clues that we're being triggered: (1) we have a sudden rush of intense emotion that leaves us feeling helpless, (2) when we tell a friend or trusted and responsible listener about the situation, he or she does not see a reason for the strong emotions, and (3) when we think back to similar situations, we see unresolved issues.

Once we realize we have been triggered, we can deal with the current situation in a mature way because the intensity dissipates.

Making Assumptions: Beverly's Story

Beverly was an adult whose developmental needs from an early age had not been met. In her work life, she often looked for rejection as a support for her earlier neglect—a kind of "I told you I am worthless." As a result, if her paycheck was not given to her at the time she expected it, she assumed it was for personal reasons. She believed she was being singled out by the human resources department. Friday afternoons became times of great anxiety and anger for her. Her angry energy led to snapping at others. Her colleagues didn't like her behavior and began to avoid her. Beverly assumed that her colleagues were banding together to hurt her. She did not see that her actions contributed to how she was being treated. In Beverly's case, her assumptions let her re-create her past neglect. This was her comfort zone.

Sometimes assumptions should be discussed with a friend. A perceived slight may be simply an oversight. E-mails do not arrive. Letters get lost. Phone messages are accidentally erased. There are many situations that we may want to ascribe a motive to that are, in fact, nothing more than the usual busyness of life.

When strong emotions arise with friends, be sure to ask questions and consider the answers against the relationship's track record. Trust is built on repeated exchanges during which questions are respectfully asked and answered.

Justifying: Larry's Story

Our emotions can be very strong, but what we think about them can be very wrong. For example, Larry has been uncommunicative emotionally for most of his ten-year marriage. His wife now wants a divorce. Larry begins to justify his silence by saying his wife was never trustworthy, that she was never committed, and that these reasons are why he couldn't open up to her. He refused counseling when she suggested it because he did not want to talk about problems. Now that the divorce is imminent, Larry refuses to go through the painful work of taking responsibility for the death of the relationship. He justifies his failures by rationalizing that she was never a good wife. He makes up stories containing half-truths to support his desire not to change.

Justifying our actions and failures to act can become habitual. These kinds of justifications can keep us from the truth, from getting unstuck, and from finding our way to new situations and happiness.

Knowing what our feelings are, easily recognizing them, and taking responsibility for them is a kind of insurance. This insurance guarantees that if and when we have difficult surprises that resurrect old feelings and add new feelings to the mix, we will know how to deal with them wisely. We will not need to control others' behavior to keep emotions at bay. And we won't need to seek revenge or act out on others who we feel are causing us grief. We won't need to find other behaviors to displace our real feelings.

HIDDEN OUTCOMES OF OUR EMOTIONAL LIVES

Emotions do not go where we tell them to go. They tell us where *they* want to go. They teach us, guide us, and help us grow up. Emotions course through our lives, and we are responsible for learning from them.

Emotions are stimulating pieces of energetic information that support our awareness, our individual growth, and our capacity for understanding. We use difficult situations to grow better lives. We become wise. We become mentors whose rich experiences are helpful to our communities.

Letting go of feelings becomes an important choice. We either choose or refuse. When we choose, we evolve. When we refuse, we lose control over our personal emotional power.

Each feeling and each circumstance has a varied energy, which may feel heavy, light, intense, airy, or dense. Labeling and becoming familiar with the shades of emotions can help us refine our ideas. We can then choose whether to act. Chapter 9, "Communication Skills," details techniques for doing this.

MOVING FORWARD

Emotions are wonderful building blocks that help us discover ourselves. They do not have to be unknown forces that impel us toward overwhelming and out-of-control fates.

When we have clarity about the nature of our emotional selves, we can navigate successfully through what might otherwise be a threatening, unknown cloud. We can use our feelings to enormous advantage. They are signposts. They are clues. They allow us the treasure of emotional understanding. They can be keys to living lovely, meaningful lives—if we let them.

The next five chapters discuss our five basic emotions, beginning with anger.

Anger

The Verboten One

Anger and sorrow are like twins; one is often found with the other. However, in our culture, anger is much more evident than sorrow. Anger typically hides other less obvious feelings, as well as those less acceptable to us—namely, feelings that reveal vulnerability. Vulnerable feelings such as sorrow and fear are often found masquerading as anger or lying behind anger. Sometimes the force of anger carries with it the energy of these other unexpressed and unrecognized emotions, and when it does, the power of anger is unequaled.

Anger has an energetic core that demands something be done! But anger also has other shapes and shades. As with any emotion, feelings of anger occur on a continuum. There can be little angers and enormous ones, old and new, justified or not, and acted on or not. Anger can be turned toward oneself (act in), or it can be turned toward others (act out).

The Anger Continuum

*Afraid of feeling or expressing anger

39

THE ENERGY OF ANGER

The energy that becomes available when we are angry can be put to good or destructive purposes. Anger can be the first push toward new ideas, growth, change, and achievement of goals. Anger can also lead to violence and addictive cycles of "power over."

Power-over situations involve one person dominating another. Power over is not concerned with respect or mutuality. Power-over relationships are based in unconscious issues of insecurity and fear. Once the anger flows out, the need to have power over diminishes temporarily until the cyclical need for security and control begins to build once again.

Anger is an important energy to become familiar with and accountable for. When we do not learn how to have a healthy relationship with anger, we suffer the most devastating consequences. For example, many crimes come from feelings of anger, especially when it is felt or expressed unexpectedly.

Anger's energy takes many forms, both negative and positive. The first step we can take toward becoming responsible for anger is to recognize that *anger has energy*. Pure and simple! We can feel it. We know it. It comes out in headaches, stomachaches, muscle tension, jaw clenching, foot tapping, gum snapping, change jangling, foot shifting, throat clearing, shoe scuffing, eye rolling, hand wringing, finger tapping, shoulder slumping, and so on. There are many ways through which we attempt to release the energy of anger.

Why is it important to acknowledge that anger has energy? When we name the energy, we become conscious of who we are in that moment, and we are no longer at the whim of a forceful emotion. The energy loses some of its push. Remember the story of *Rumpelstiltskin?* Rumpelstiltskin had helped a girl to become queen, and in exchange, he demanded she give him her first-born son. The queen thought the little man would forget. But after her baby was born, Rumpelstiltskin showed up and demanded the queen's son. The queen was frightened. The little man said that unless the queen called him by his right name, she would have to forfeit her child. The queen asked for help and got it from a "messenger." The little man showed up for the last time, and the queen called him by his right name. When the little man heard his real name, he vanished forever. Similarly, when we name our feelings, we release them and their energy. And as the queen became wiser as a result of her experience, so will we.

Change occurs when we name our emotions as we feel them. In telling the truth, energy is released.

EXPRESSIONS OF ANGER

Once we begin to notice the energy of our anger, we can increase our awareness about how we express it. We express anger in two ways: (1) acting out and (2) acting in.

Acting Out

Acting out often seems natural enough. As babies, some of us learn that we can get what we want by acting out. We scream, hit, and throw tantrums. If we are not taught anything else, we will continue to act out simply because it seems to work, at least in the short run.

Acting out means that when we feel anger, we believe we are entitled to take the energy out on something or someone else. Doing so can escalate powerful feelings in both parties. At some point, we may enter a kind of *anger trance.* While in the trance, we stop thinking, we see red instead of other options, and we attempt to inflict the force of our emotions on the other person. Of course, this can be appropriate when our lives are imperiled. But most of the time, we are not in life-and-death situations. Generally, acting out is not an effective method for resolving differences.

The Steps to Avoid Acting Out

Step one requires looking at our beliefs. What beliefs do we have that support our acting out? Do we believe that if we have uncomfortable feelings, someone else must be to blame? If someone is to blame, must we punish that person? Is it up to us to decide on the punishment? If we look closely at this train of thought, we might see how similar it is to a child's belief system. When children act out, we say they do not know better. We teach them how to grow up. When adults act out, we say they should know better. We put abusive men and women in jail. When there is willingness, belief systems and behaviors can be changed, whether the person is a child or an adult.

Step two involves becoming aware of our triggers: words, actions, and situations that annoy us. I know a couple who tended to have arguments before dinner. Once they realized they were eating meals long after their blood-sugar level had fallen, they learned to either snack as soon as they got home from work or set the dinner hour earlier. Their arguing had to do with a situational trigger. Noticing the pattern let them become aware and make changes.

Step three is about noticing the progression of our anger. We begin noticing when we *first* become angry. For example, we take note of small angers as they occur, such as an unresolved run-in with a colleague, getting stuck in traffic on our way home, and annoyance at the hot weather. We acknowledge them to ourselves—"I am so angry with my co-worker. I hate sitting in traffic. This heat just wears me out!"—so that by the time we walk into our home, we don't explode needlessly or take our frustration and anger out on our family. We watch ourselves as anger builds and we try to do something about releasing it right away. We can be creative: yell in the car, call someone for coffee, or pull over and talk things out on the phone. When we get home, we can ask the children to play outside while we take ten minutes to share our day with another adult.

Step four involves thinking about the patterns of events and triggers that cause us to become angry. The patterns may have to do with external events, such as environmental factors in our work situation. Or the patterns may have to do with our internal habits, such as taking the actions of others personally. If we see a pattern, we can choose to interrupt it. For example, we may talk with a colleague. We may drive a different route home. We may take a day off to rest. We may include more supports in our day, such as going to lunch with a friend or planning a date with our spouse. We are not always required to take care of the situation ourselves nor are we required to do so immediately.

We could also choose not to interrupt the pattern. In this case, we acknowledge the anger and give ourselves outlets for releasing the energy. For example, we can exercise or get involved in a sport, channel the energy into our personal goals or hobbies, or do something creative such as drawing or playing an instrument. And we can use our emotional inventories to release the underlying, long-standing, undischarged anger (see "Taking an Emotional Inventory" on pages 163–167).

Even if we can't stop being angry, we can lessen the amount of energy we carry by following the four steps explained above:

1. look at our beliefs
2. define our triggers
3. notice the progression of our anger
4. think about patterns that cause anger and choose what we can do to change either the situation or ourselves

When we act out, we have not taken the necessary steps to address our anger. We are unable to articulate our underlying beliefs. We do not notice a buildup. We are not aware of multiple reactions. We do not take responsibility for reactions. We may even like the feeling because we want the power associated with it. We may gravitate toward situations and people we can dominate. Acting out produces short-lived satisfaction.

How Do We Act Out?

Some typical physical ways of acting out are pounding, hitting, punching, beating, clenching, staring down, giving someone the finger, bullying, using weapons or objects as weapons, stealing, making sexual advances, being reckless to intimidate or scare, threatening with fists or objects, and killing.

Some typical verbal ways of acting out are daring others, getting in their faces, yelling, shouting, screaming, gossiping, teasing, taunting, demeaning, using slurs, swearing, using sexual language, baiting, blackmailing, denying, and pretending not to understand.

The Benefits of Acting Out

When we make a habit of acting out, we get something from doing it. Otherwise we would stop. Here is a sample list of benefits:

- releasing energy
- having power over someone
- feeling superior
- getting what we want
- making others act/behave in ways that let us stay in our comfort zone
- punishing, getting revenge, or paying back

- making ourselves feel "better than" by trying to make others feel "less than"
- trying to get others to feel as miserable as we do

The Consequences of Acting Out

When we act out, we experience a host of emotional consequences. For example, if we are angry, come home, and beat up our spouse or children, we may get rid of some of our angry energy, but we've also created more angry energy in the form of self-hatred. And we've given those we love a reason to be angry back. Additionally, there are legal consequences because we have committed a crime. Acting out may prevent us from

- getting close to people
- trusting others and ourselves, and from being considered trustworthy
- letting others love us
- being open to change, new possibilities, learning, insights, growth, and maturity
- feeling self-love, self-worth, and hope
- being able to live in our home with our children
- having healthy relationships with our children
- associating with friends and family

Acting Out: Judy's Story

I had a good first impression of Judy. She was friendly and interesting. At some point, we went to a workshop together on counseling parents who abuse children. I watched her from across the room as she obviously tried to get the male speaker's attention. She was a woman in her late twenties. She sat on the floor while most of us were in chairs. She hiked her skirt up and exposed her underwear throughout the seminar. Later, when I asked her why she did these things, she said she wanted to make the male instructor nervous. She had no sexual interest in him. She did not know him. But she had a past that included sexual powerlessness. In this innocuous and safe situation, she had found a way to get back at her past through an innocent instructor. She saw it as neither angry nor negative. It was her way of getting revenge. She did it consciously and without regard for the consequences. I was stunned then and am again today thinking about it: how we perpetrate our unclaimed emotional lives on others, who then must either deal with them or put these unclaimed feelings on yet another's heart.

Unexpected Anger

Unexpected anger "attacks" combine surprise with forceful energy for the person having them and the person they erupt on. These attacks are brought on by *emotional land mines,* usually triggered by innocent parties. We can also think of them as *lightning strikes*—where friend or foe might accidentally trigger old hurts that result in lightning-quick responses. When we get caught off guard in this state, we may feel ripped by an emotional explosion that resurrects every bit of previously unresolved emotion. It suddenly spews out of that big unclaimed murky pool. A huge wave engulfs us, and we are suddenly carried off in its energy. We overreact. We are irrational. We say and do things not typical of us. And often, the person who triggers it is totally innocent.

When unexpected anger arises, we can use the four steps described earlier. We can exercise some choice over how we allow our angry energy to surface. We can use each episode of unexpected anger as a way to change how we overreact. We can learn to modify our belief system about who is responsible for our emotions and our actions.

Acting In

Acting in means turning our angry energy back onto ourselves. This anger can become destructive and lead to silent self-hatred that may grow to the point of suicide. Turning anger inside can be lethal.

Just as some of us were taught that acting out is effective, others have been taught that it is safer to keep anger inside, that we are more lovable if we are "nice" and silent. This takes a tremendous toll because the more we hold back, the more we shred our relationship with ourselves. Every time we neglect our instincts, we create regret, frustration, and helplessness—all of which lead to stress.

The Steps to Avoid Acting In

Step one is, again, related to our beliefs. Do we think that holding back anger protects others? Do we believe that experiencing anger will cause us to reel out of control and harm someone? Do we think that if we let others know we're angry, they'll have information about how to really "push our buttons"? Or will they leave us? Were we told not to get angry? Do we consider anger a "sin"? Were we punished for our anger? There are many beliefs that can lead to taking anger out on ourselves.

Step two is about noticing the progression of our anger. We may shut down legitimate reactions to being violated in order not to become angry. What triggers our holding on to anger? Do we suppress, hold back, or squash the very beginnings of anger by denying how we feel or are affected? We may tell ourselves, "It's not that important," when the incident *is* important to us. We can start to notice when we begin to shut off or shut down our reactions.

Once we notice, step three involves giving ourselves permission to experience anger. Being safe in the midst of feeling angry is key. We try on anger in safety by understanding that anger is an energy that's neither bad nor good. We practice seeing that it is how we *express* anger that determines whether anger is harmful or helpful. We notice that anger is helpful because it can point to someone's lack of respect for us, or it may convey our likes and dislikes. We allow the reality of what annoys us to become conscious.

Step four is about changing our framework of self-blame. Instead of asking why someone was disrespectful, we begin by calling the feeling by name and using "I" in the expressing of emotion: "I am a little bit angry that my boss didn't give me a bonus this year." At this point, we aren't blaming the boss. We are just letting ourselves know where the feelings are coming from.

Step five is working toward sharing our feelings and thoughts with another person, instead of grasping on to them. We ask a friend if we can practice what we'd like to say to the boss. We write what we might want to say. We think of what we will gain from telling the truth and what we may lose. We look at our fears with regard to the consequences. We check out with someone else whether our fears are founded. We eventually become able to talk about what we need and want with the appropriate person.

Then, in step six, we choose how to release the angry feeling. If we choose not to act on it, then we can release the energy by telling someone else we feel angry. Or we can combine the emotion with an action, like sweeping, while we have an internal conversation with the boss. Or we can write an angry letter and then burn it. But if we choose to act on the anger, then we may calmly go to the boss as soon as possible and share our reasons for thinking we deserved the bonus. We are specific and are able to support our wants and needs.

Admitting that others have a responsibility to treat us with respect is a belief that empowers us in judging whether our boundaries are being invaded. After we make that assessment, then we choose what to do next.

Again, even if we can't completely stop holding back anger, we can increase our access to it and lessen the amount of energy we silently carry. We can help ourselves by following the six steps explained above:

1. look at our beliefs
2. notice the progression of our anger
3. give ourselves permission to experience anger
4. change our self-blame to self-responsibility
5. share our feelings and thoughts with another person
6. choose how to release the angry feeling

How Do We Act In?

Some typical physical ways of acting in are smoking, drinking, drugging, cutting ourselves, overdosing, eating too little, eating too much, keeping company with dangerous people, putting ourselves in dangerous situations, attempting suicide, feeling depressed, not taking sexual safety precautions, and being in unhealthy relationships.

Some typical verbal ways of acting in are saying nothing, blaming ourselves, saying "I don't care" when we do care, lying, manipulating, acting "as if," pretending to be someone we are not, focusing on others' needs instead of our own, "understanding" others as an excuse for accepting their abusive behaviors, being phobic about saying "no," withholding, pulling away, giving in to the demands of others due to our fear of being angry, and refusing to admit that something or someone is causing us fear, pain, or sorrow.

The Benefits of Acting In

There are lots of benefits for acting in too. By doing so, we think we're punishing others. Saying "I'll show you" or "I don't care" to ourselves are clues that we're acting in, especially when followed by a self-abusive behavior. Self-blame is tough to let go of when we won't let anyone in. Like shame, self-blame has no answer to the "why" question. When we ask ourselves *why* we are being treated in a disrespectful or abusive way, the typical answer we give ourselves is "I must have done something wrong." In other words, we think "I deserve it."

As with acting out, we experience certain benefits when we act in:

- looking competent and in control even when we aren't
- keeping our vulnerability secret, maybe even from ourselves
- keeping distance from our spouse or partner, so our love is flawed without real risk to us
- not having to develop the negotiation skills necessary to find our way in life
- not asking for what we want or need, so we can secretly blame others for our unspent life
- not having to go through the work of creating a healthy self-knowledge

And so, if we act in, we cannot be truly known by others or ourselves and, thus, not truly loved. In not being loved, we stay within our comfort zone—unchanging.

By keeping silent about how we really feel and think, we may be able to pretend we have no wants or needs that will inconvenience other people. By pretending, we can hold on to relationships with those who mean more to us than we do to ourselves. We may be willing to pay the high cost of lying in order to "get" someone we want, but this someone can never love whom he or she does not truly know.

The Consequences of Acting In

There are consequences for acting in, even though they may be a bit subtler than those for acting out. While being angry with ourselves doesn't seem to hurt anyone, a closer look shows physical and emotional consequences. Being angry with ourselves or holding on to anger can manifest physically and cause problems such as heart or immune system ailments. Other consequences of acting in include

- being very alone in our lives
- teaching others it is okay to mistreat us
- teaching others that we matter less than they do
- denying ourselves in the outside world while harboring pressing needs inside to the point of being passive-aggressive to get our way
- teaching others, whether children, co-workers, bosses, or family members, that they do not need to be responsible for their behavior
- teaching others to depend on us when we do not depend on ourselves
- having a false sense of emotional stability or serenity

The difference between *being selfless* and *acting as if we are selfless* comes from our intent. When we deny ourselves out of fear, we create layers of unmet needs. It is okay to have a healthy selfishness and to take care of ourselves. Give-and-take is necessary.

When we are selfless, we are able to forgo the overt reward and give unconditionally. We realize that we matter just as much as others, but we don't need the attention as a reward. Those who are able to do this as a lifestyle are often highly evolved spiritually. They have gone through the stages of setting boundaries, saying "no," and taking care of themselves.

Most of us know when we're being passive-aggressive, such as when we are habitually late, change the rules, forget to keep promises, or make up gossip and spread it under the guise of concern.

Acting In: Kit's Story

Kit considered himself a good person. He was invested in making sure that others also thought him a good person. His list of shoulds included never getting angry with anyone. He defined himself as being generous and nice. His belief was that anger was unnecessary and that, in fact, it was wrong to have feelings of anger. When his girlfriend cheated on him and broke up with him, he thought it must have been his fault. He forgave her.

Later, when Kit became interested in a new relationship with a woman named Patricia, he encouraged her to depend on his financial support for her and her son. Over time, Kit began finding it hard to meet Patricia's growing requests for money. He blamed himself for not earning enough money. When Patricia told Kit her son's needs were being neglected, Kit felt even more helpless. He loved Patricia and her son, and he was becoming afraid that she would cheat on him.

The more invested Kit became in Patricia, the less he

thought of himself. When Patricia cheated on him, Kit became suicidal. Friends and family finally recognized Kit's distress and were able to help him.

AVOIDING ANGER

Some of us cannot even get to the point of feeling angry. What happens when we are too scared by the intensity of our anger to do anything about it? This is called *anger phobia.* The fear of being overwhelmed by angry feelings can be paralyzing. Some of us stay locked up. Even acting out our emotional lives in the safety of a counseling session is too threatening. There is professional help for those terrified of being angry.

Saving angry feelings for a rainy day, putting them off, avoiding them, shifting them onto someone else, denying them—while convenient for the moment—does not work in the long run. These methods break down, and eventually the anger does come out—at the wrong time and at the wrong person. Or anger gets internalized and creates physical problems, such as headaches, backaches, heart problems, or even cancer. These can wear down the immune system and lead to other serious illnesses. In addition, when we avoid our anger,

- we don't really know who we are
- we don't mature
- we keep others at a distance
- we deny ourselves the validity of our lives

Whether acting out, acting in, or avoiding, these wayward expressions of anger are ineffective because we are not freed from the energy connected to the feeling. Only a true matching of feeling to situation releases the energy.

USING ANGER TO OUR BENEFIT

Now that we've discussed the various expressions of anger, we can turn to *how to make changes* that will take us slowly toward a different way of responding.

The Old Way of Getting Angry	A New Way
We feel angry.	We take responsibility for our anger by saying to ourselves, "I feel angry."
We blame someone else for our anger.	We realize that we'll feel more powerful if we let the blame stage pass and then work on a solution.
We react, either verbally or physically, by acting in or acting out.	We use the angry energy to ask questions. We hold the energy in check to further our understanding, make a plan, and figure out our options. We use the energy to call a friend to ask for help.
The other person gets mad at us in return, sometimes being unaware of how his or her behavior originally provoked us.	If someone intentionally tried to make us angry, we do not escalate. We leave her or him with personal discomfort and make plans to resolve our emotional reaction in our own time and way. If someone unintentionally aroused our anger, we discuss the interaction and work with it.
The argument escalates until the parties get worn out by doing their typical behavior.	If the other's behavior was unintentional, there is greater understanding and closeness. If the

	other's behavior was intentional, we keep our self-respect and use the available energy to further our own lives. We choose.
The cycle is repeated.	Old patterns that brought distance are replaced by mutually helpful patterns that cause important relationships to flourish.

WHEN WE SUCCESSFULLY SHARE ANGRY FEELINGS RESPONSIBLY

The person on the receiving end of our responsible attitudes may give us clues about the genuineness and success of our sharing. In listening to us, the other person may suddenly feel the clarity that comes when we understand another's motives. That clarity can be poignant. The other person might feel moved that we took the time or were willing to be vulnerable and honest. When we risk saying "It was my fault," powerful moments of respect and love often follow. Someone who had been left to wonder about our actions and motives may release harbored fears and anger. This person may forgive us or tell us he or she understands. Nonthreatening honesty about anger carries the seeds for deeper trust and stronger ties. Clearing up misunderstandings restores and leavens our relationships. Sharing angry feelings responsibly enables powerful, durable, and beneficial results.

ANGER EXERCISES

You will find directions for an emotional inventory on pages 163–167. The questions will help release emotional energy for each feeling, and the inventory is especially useful in clearing away old emotional energy.

The exercises below are meant to help you specifically with anger that is more current. If you want to start establishing your emotional vocabulary, read over all the exercises here and start tomorrow with a new awareness of your emotions. Use a notebook designated just for learning about your emotions. Put your exercises in this one place so you can see both your patterns and your solutions over time.

1. Think about your day in order to increase your awareness of feeling angry. Did you hold back how you felt at some point or did you say something you now regret due to your angry feelings? If so, write down what happened. Where were you? What was said? What was the end result? Where did your feelings go? Where might you be holding this emotional energy in your body? Write out what you might have said if you had owned how you felt. You don't need to say this directly to the person who triggered the emotional event. The point is to own how you feel and see how you habitually deal with your angry reactions.

2. For a period of two days, list each event where you act in or act out. Simply list the events and the feelings you have. Is there a pattern in the people involved? Is there a pattern in the circumstances?

3. Keep a journal for one week or plan a daily call-in time (no more than ten minutes) with a friend for one week, during which you note when angry feelings get triggered, whether you own them, whether you deal with them appropriately, or whether you store them. Then make a wish list for what you would like to do. For example:

May 25: I felt angry at work because my supervisor canceled my job review for the second time. Instead of letting her know I felt angry, I snapped at a co-worker. Now I am angry with myself.

Wish: Next time, I will go to my supervisor and say, "Sallie, I feel angry that you have canceled my job review. I need feedback about my job performance. Let's make a time to meet sometime today." And I will apologize to my colleague tomorrow.

4. If you try some of the approaches explained in this chapter, note how you feel, how the other person seemed to take your words, and where your energy went.
5. When did you "dump" on someone else? Was this person known to you or was he or she a stranger? Older or younger? Related to your anger reasons or totally unrelated? Friend or enemy? Female or male? Do you notice any patterns in your "dumping"? Who's taking the brunt? Why them and not someone else? Make a decision to acknowledge but also hold on to your anger for a day, in order to plan a responsible reaction. Make a decision to be as respectful as possible to the other person. Note how not immediately acting on your feelings affects you. Give yourself credit for that day. Give yourself ways to release emotions. Try talking, exercising, doing chores, and having a conversation with yourself. Yell when you are alone in the house or ask a friend to listen to you yell. Creating artwork, storytelling, dancing, and writing music or poetry are all methods that transform energy. Try various methods to see which ones work well for you. Keep adding days until you have a good handle on this method as a viable option.

Sometimes it takes us more than a single effort to release layers of emotion, but with practice, it becomes much easier.

MOVING FORWARD

If we look at unhelpful patterns and create new scenarios, eventually our new methods change from stiff to naturally flowing responses. We will notice a lessening of our need to lash out or hold back. We may find forgiving easier. And we will find lots more energy to use in following our inclinations.

Later in this book, there are many opportunities to check out how emotional awareness and responsibility free us up. Eventually, the emotional ingredients in many of our reactions become clear quickly. We spend less and less time in endless cycles of arguing and wondering why it's always about the same things. We move to a new stage in our relationships with the world and with ourselves.

The next chapter details how much of our energy we use just to keep fear at bay.

FIVE

Fear

A Vulnerable Ability

This chapter should not be skipped over. In fact, the less we want to read and use the information in this chapter, the more we may need it. Fear loves to hide behind other emotions, such as anger, and shifts from being obvious to covert, as in when we avoid situations and people. Being reluctant to read this chapter or dismissing the content before giving it a chance may be clues about the role fear plays in our lives.

The Fear Continuum

uneasy	nervous	tense	jumpy	restless	worried
					apprehensive
paralyzed	terrified	panicked	scared	alarmed	anxious

ABOUT FEAR

Fears can be big, small, realistic, imagined, expected, and unexpected. Fear can be general (being afraid of closed-in spaces like elevators) or specific (being afraid of a big dog). We can project future fears and dwell on past fears. This is an unwieldy emotion.

Fear, like other emotions, gives us information when we

connect its energy to its origins—whether person, place, idea, value, belief, event, or institution. Naming the fear releases some of the energy. Fear differs from other emotions in that we often need to substitute new thoughts, behaviors, interpretations, and meanings about events and people in order to override the fear and move on.

There are many reasonable fears based on the need for safety in which an action is necessary to resolve the problem. This chapter deals, for the most part, with fear issues that are not so easily resolved.

THE ENERGY OF FEAR

The energy of fear can be shocking, like shards of glass or stabs of electricity, such as waking from a nightmare or hearing bad news. Or fear can come in a whisper not to walk down a certain street. Fear gives us jitters when we feel nervous about taking risks or trying new possibilities. Fear's energy is palpable. Sometimes the energy is useful, as when we're preparing for a sports competition. Sometimes the energy is paralyzing, as when we're about to speak in public and find no words available.

Retrieving energy from past fear is a paradox because we must feel relatively safe in order to re-experience and release the fear. Fear, even from the past, can return in full force when we recall it. We may find ourselves *in* the fear, rather than objectively outside it. This intense reaction serves its purpose as long as the fear is real and immediate. But ongoing fear carried after the threat is gone creates difficulties.

Ongoing fear is not always inactive. It can grow offshoots and spread, as well as create layers of blocked energy. But we can unravel the road map of fear and get the important messages our fears hold. We release and heal from the fear by telling our stories and making conscious choices to confront, override, or substitute ideas and actions for old responses, as necessary. We can move on. The clues we find when exploring our fears can point us in rich new directions toward healing, eliminating generational family issues, and pursuing other interests.

FEARS BEYOND THE SCOPE OF THIS BOOK

Some fears do not fall into the self-help range. Paralyzing, terrifying fears and intrusive anxiety disorders that are genetic and/or biochemical in nature need professional intervention. *This book is not intended to cover clinical information. Please consult a health professional.* Fears that can be alleviated, understood, and released through self-understanding and discovery are the focus of this chapter.

WHAT SCARES US?

Fears are subjective and changeable. What one person finds frightening, another finds exciting. But most of us would agree that self-generated fearful experiences are easier to tolerate than those that surprise us from external sources. Self-generated purposeful fears are those we choose to go through in order to reach personal goals, like getting to the exhilaration stage of hang gliding. We know, in advance, that fear will be a stage in the process. We have some control over the situation. And we can choose to forgo the experience if we have a change of heart.

Fear caused externally, not generated or controlled by us, brings surprise. These fears leave us to find meaning in them *after* the fact. We don't get to choose. When companies fold, we may fear for our finances, job security, and all that goes with it. We have choices in how we deal with fear afterward, but we don't have foresight or choice about whether we feel afraid.

And being caught off guard is often what we find almost as distasteful as the event itself.

OUR FIRST PHYSICAL RESPONSE TO FEAR

Whether fear is created by us or not, the body reacts in basically the same way. Fear causes the body to release adrenaline: a neurotransmitter released in response to stress, which sends blood to muscles, arteries, and the brain. When the provocative situation is short lived, our bodies become empowered to resolve it, whether by performing superhuman feats in emergencies or by meeting tight deadlines, winning competitions, or avoiding car accidents.

Adrenaline is meant for short-term problem solving. However, if fear gets out of balance and becomes chronic, as it may for those living in dangerous neighborhoods, experiencing combat, or living in abusive situations, our bodies are given a nearly impossible task. Chronic fear tells the body to stay in a constant state of alertness. Our bodies do not differentiate between worrying, reliving the past, or actually needing adrenaline. What happens when we stay on high alert for a long time? Some of us become hypervigilant to the point of wearing out our health. Untreated chronic fears may result in high blood pressure, memory loss, ulcers, and immune system problems.

So, we need to relieve ourselves of this state. We can find ways to contain and release our fears. We can start by understanding how adrenaline works and learning about typical fear responses.

THE PROCESS OF FEAR

Adrenaline Snapshots: The Body's Photo Album

When we are surprised by the onset of a threatening circumstance, we consider it a shock to our system. The shock from the original reaction leaves biochemical traces, or *imprints*, which may remain active in our bodies for a long time, even for years. The imprinting preserves information for our protection, warning us when we are in the same realm of danger. The memory of the specific event, as well as associated parts of the adrenaline *snapshot,* can trigger reactions over and over again— as though we are living the fear in a time warp.

When the event involves survival, we go on emergency cruise control, which alerts all body systems to prepare for battle. We begin operating on reflex and instinct. Senses overload with impulses picked up from the environment while nerves deliver messages, make plans, and keep body systems, from heart to extremities, turned on and protected. We pick up whatever is in the environment through sight, sound, smell, touch, and taste and filter messages instantaneously to get the solution. The system also records all this input, like pictures in a photo album. After the event, we hold on to information from our senses and thoughts that consciously and unconsciously we believe will keep us safe next time. Sometimes what we hold on to may not be helpful in the long run, as we will see in Mariah's story.

Mariah's Fear

As a teenager, Mariah was bitten by a brown and black dog. As an adult, she reacts each time she sees a dog. If she doesn't deal with her reaction to that past event, Mariah may also begin to generalize her fear to other black and brown animals, such as cats or chipmunks. Eventually, she could begin to react to the environment where she sees cats or chipmunks, for example, at the park. By the time Mariah starts to fear grass—because her mind would associate grass with parks—she would have forgotten all about the dog.

Ways of Responding to Fear

Typically, our responses to fear can be categorized in the following way:

- We may fight, physically or verbally.
- We may flee, which can mean that we literally run away or shut down emotionally.
- We may freeze, which means we do nothing initially. When we eventually get away, we decide how to handle our fear.

There is another possible response: asking for help from a friend. Whether we are able to do this before, during, or after the event, asking for help dissipates energy.

Intervening in the Process of Fear

When we carefully consider the process of fear and our responses, we can intervene at various times to limit the consequences.

Stage of Fear	Intervention
An event causes fear.	We do what we can to avoid dangerous situations outside of our control.
We react by fighting, fleeing, or freezing.	We assess which reactions work and which don't.
We try to forget the event or get over the episode, but we revert instead to cycling through the fear or stimuli related to the fear. We do not move on.	After the event (this may be days or years), we review the event in a safe environment.

We tell ourselves that we're weak and cowardly, and we blame ourselves for being unable to "fix" the problem.	We don't judge ourselves. We make a decision to see what we can discover about ourselves in the cycle. We determine to work through to a solution in safety, with or without help.
We begin to distrust ourselves as well as the world and experience a domino-like effect of expanding situations, people, and objects to fear.	We trust that we will find a solution and become willing to try out various options, including specific actions, thoughts, and beliefs that will override or lessen fear responses.
Our world begins to narrow, and we suffer. We may lose relationships, jobs, our community, and our independence.	We determine that we will keep ourselves focused on positive outcomes, regardless of the impulse to give in. We do this through asking for help and staying involved with others.
Our fear begins to contaminate our daily lives, and we lose touch with what we may legitimately fear.	We contain our fears through practice, and we begin to lose our fears and trust our instincts because we are staying in touch with reality and releasing our ties to old stimuli.

Regardless of our response, we must continually assess whether the fear is a new fear or a chronic fear. How do we tell the difference? The next section looks at fears—physical, emotional, social, and spiritual—and how we interpret and find meaning in them. In knowing more about how we react, we can lessen the consequences of our fear.

TYPES OF FEAR

Physical (Concrete) Fear

Fears caused by concrete realities, such as being chased, intrude to help us. Physical fears run the gamut from being afraid of getting beaten up, mugged, or hit to fears of falling down stairs, having a car accident, or being diagnosed with an incurable illness. The "not knowing" aspect of these fears drives us until we have the facts. Once we know what's going to happen (for example, after we have fallen and are in the hospital with a cast and prognosis), adrenaline is no longer necessary.

Even with the element of surprise and the unknown outcomes, our reactions to physical fear are shaped through anticipation, revisiting, and practice. For example, we can teach ourselves how to control our breathing (on our own or through the use of biofeedback equipment). We can learn how to relax despite feeling alarmed (through yoga, meditation, and breathing exercises). We can consider whether to run (through anticipating possibilities and preparing for them).

We can short-circuit old fear by choosing nontriggering thoughts. First, we discover the exact thoughts and cues that trigger the old fear. Second, we change our interpretations because the event is in the past. Third, we replace our old interpretations by walking through the situation literally or figuratively. And last, we add new comforting interpretations or messages that override the old.

No matter what the fear is, whether big or little, old or new, real or imagined, we can change our response. And while we may not be able to refrain from being surprised and scared initially, we can choose whether we stay in fight, flight, or freeze mode.

Leah's Fear

Leah's three-year-old son Lorenzo was very active. She loved him so much! His eyes were always darting around the apartment looking for the next object to explore. Leah would not let anyone babysit for him because she believed that a sitter wouldn't be able to anticipate Lorenzo's curiosity and quickness.

One morning, Leah was taking a walk around the neighborhood with her son. As a friend came around the corner, so did her German shepherd, which broke from its leash and ran at them with unfriendly barking. Lorenzo, terrified, slipped from his mother's hand and darted into the busy street. Oncoming traffic abruptly screeched to a halt as Lorenzo ran. Leah leaped across the two lanes of cars without thinking. Her heart felt as though it would jump out of her skin. After getting Lorenzo safely back into her arms, Leah burst into tears.

In this situation, adrenaline helped Leah instantly assess her choices and make a split-second decision to run after her son, instead of battling the dog or considering her own safety. Lorenzo used adrenaline to run away from the dog. And afterward, when they were safe, Leah released more of her pent-up energy through tears.

Now that Leah and her son are safe, she can make some decisions. She knows that her son will run from unfriendly dogs. She can teach her son to jump into her arms the next time he's afraid. She can teach Lorenzo how to approach animals that are friendly. And Leah can model her fearlessness by continuing to take walks with Lorenzo that will have other outcomes. In this way, they will both form new responses.

Emotional (Abstract) Fear

Emotional fears are the results of our thoughts and ideas, which affect us in myriad ways. Sometimes the fears are immediate and overt, such as fear about losing a relationship. Others are covert and have become unclear over time, such as fear of rejection. Uncovering the sources of long-standing fear can bring us self-understanding and compassion for others and ourselves. It can also help us release the adaptations we have made in our lives to accommodate fears created in the distant past. We can release many emotional fears if we complete the fear inventory in "Taking an Emotional Inventory" (pages 163–167).

Dwayne's Fear

Dwayne, who would like to be in a relationship, is afraid of rejection. Without consciously knowing why, Dwayne has created a belief system from childhood that equates "no" with rejection. He has come to believe that "no" means "I'm not good enough" or "I'm unlovable." His fears of not being good enough may be a family-inspired belief he created to explain to himself why his parents said "no." Taking a risk with a potential "no" answer now has tremendous power to keep Dwayne from accomplishing his heart's desires.

Dwayne has let habit replace possibility. He no longer sees that perhaps "No, I can't go out with you" might mean the person is busy, already dating someone, or refusing his offer for her own reasons. Each time a woman refuses to go out on a date with him, Dwayne fears that he is not "good enough."

He Says	She Says	He Hears	She Means
Hello, Serena, are you interested in going to a movie on Friday night?	I'd like to, but I'm busy.	She doesn't like me.	I'm busy that night.

Dwayne's thought process successfully postpones rejection but also postpones his ability to get to the source of his fear. Emotional fears point to information about ourselves, as well as to the creative ways in which we can release them.

Social and Spiritual Fears

Social and spiritual fears, while perhaps not life threatening, are important to take stock of because they can become sources of chronic worry. Social fears have to do with the face, or persona, we present to the world. Spiritual fears often have to do with an unforgiving or humanlike understanding of God, onto which we project our life experiences.

Social fears are fairly easy to see and access, and they are often quite visible to others. Social fears include fears about how we look ("What will they think of my new haircut?") and fears of inadequacy ("I'm not making enough money to get a new SUV"). We feel insecure ("I don't have enough education"), so we try to control others or situations ("I won't get that promotion unless I make him look bad"). We may gossip out of fear that we aren't legitimate in our own right ("Did you know that she failed her exam?"). Fears often hide in negative attitudes ("All men are cheaters, so I can't date"). And the fear that we can't achieve our dreams pushes us to manipulate others ("Why would anyone want to take up a musical instrument?").

These fears are about "losing face," making mistakes, looking bad, being different, being judged, failing or succeeding, being powerless or powerful, losing money, not making enough money, or failing to succeed publicly. These types of fears can serve us well because we can do something with the resulting energy. There is no emergency! Many times the only thing holding us back from using energy related to social fears is our lack of awareness that fear is the motivating factor.

Spiritual fears can be inventoried and discussed with spiritual advisors. These fears are best dealt with through the eyes, ears, and heart of a spiritual advisor who has a reputation for supporting our spiritual lives rather than punishing us. Ask around to determine who fits the bill. The last things we need in the midst of a spiritual emergency are platitudes and punishments.

Fear and Dave's Persona

Dave is a successful businessman. He meets the public easily and negotiates big money deals. At home, he is not so impenetrable. He has a weak ego when it comes to his wife. He becomes jealous if other men look at her. He tells her he wants her all to himself. His wife has grown uncomfortable when going to dinner because her husband makes a scene if the waiter seems too friendly.

Dave's ego suffers when his wife is given attention. Instead of seeing this issue as a personal wake-up call to look at his fear and his need to control, Dave is focusing instead on the other person, a waiter, who is just doing his job.

In this case, Dave's fears are part of his belief system. For him, being successful means dominating negotiations, being in charge, and controlling conversations. Dave is good at his job because he is driven to do well. In public, when other men are friendly to his wife, Dave sees this as a failure to control others, to dominate, to be in charge. He doesn't see that it is inappropriate to use business skills in a social situation or at home with the woman he loves. His fears are basic internal insecurities that he is either unaware of or chooses to keep outside himself because it is easier not to be vulnerable.

WORKING WITH FEAR

Now that we know something about types of fear and typical response modes, we can consider another set of factors: whether
the fear is here and now, in the past, or in the future. Then we
can begin making plans for working with our fears.

Time	Emotional Fear	Spiritual Fear	Social Fear	Physical Fear
Current	Afraid I won't get the loan.	Afraid I am being punished.	Afraid of getting close.	Afraid this person is going to hurt me.
Past	Afraid of being re-jected, like I was before.	Afraid God doesn't love me.	Afraid I have noth-ing to offer.	Afraid I'll be attacked again if I go out alone at night.
Future	What if I don't get the loan?	What if I am going to hell?	What if I am always alone?	What if someone hurts me?

As we can see, there is a lot of thinking that goes along with
fear. If we take some time to look at whether or not the fear is
justified, we can further evaluate how we tie our energy up in
fear. For example, we can take the fear "What if I don't get the
loan?" and answer the question. What is the worst thing that
could happen? If we don't get the loan, maybe we won't move
when we want to. Do we have other options? How much time do
we want to spend thinking about this? Is it time to let go and
allow the situation to evolve? When we consider these factors,

we're able to make a judgment (a little bit of fear is justified, but the fear itself is adding nothing to getting the loan) and a decision (time to let the fear go). We can then consciously let go of the fear.

With smaller worries, sometimes just listing them during stressful times will show us what we can let go of. It can be a relief for us to acknowledge there is nothing more we can do.

We can release many of our fears by using an inventory like the one on pages 163–167. We look for patterns. We notice what sets us off. We examine the patterns and triggers in our fears. Once we know what these are, we make choices about where we focus our thoughts and hearts. When we identify our fears, we can make plans for managing them. We can use techniques like *flooding* (turning our physical and emotional focus everywhere but on the fear). We can also give ourselves relief through spiritual practices and activities that soothe us or release our jitters, such as exercising, talking, going to the movies, taking classes, going to support meetings, reading, and finding new interests. (A set of exercises for managing and releasing fears is at the end of this chapter.)

When fear doesn't release easily, we unravel it, figure out the beliefs that support it, and then choose to live by new beliefs. For example, if we are afraid of the dark, we ask ourselves what we believe about the dark. We get to the core of our belief, which may be that the dark makes us close to invisible and, therefore, at risk of disappearing. We recognize this as a childhood belief and then carefully find a substitution for this belief. We might, for instance, choose to believe that we will not disappear in the dark, that we are real, important, and well loved. Then we can practice overriding the fear by walking through a dark room while repeating our new belief to ourselves. Over time, we can override the previous belief. If it's too threatening to do alone, we ask a friend to "spot" us while we practice.

When fears are too threatening to even consider confronting, we seek professional help.

Fears are sometimes caused by a lack of essential nutrition. Be sure to see a doctor and a nutritionist for a thorough medical workup.

Professional Options for Clearing Cyclical Fear

Traditional therapy lets us discover much about ourselves, our families, and generational fears, as well as how to deal with or avoid fear. Therapy teaches us the steps to take toward filling in developmental gaps related to fear. Many times, just exploring the fears and talking about the events are enough to establish balance.

If fears are causing panic attacks that are in a pattern of escalation, sometimes the best treatment is to stop the escalation first and work on the underlying origins later. There are several therapeutic techniques that work very well to stop the pattern of escalation, such as cognitive-behavioral therapy and therapies that clear the event, through either energy work (energy psychology) or programming (neuro-linguistic programming).

Briefly, these treatments create new information at the site where fearful thoughts previously existed. By pairing new thoughts with body responses, the body and mind work together to override the fear by creating new, nonfearful associations. We replace our body's interpretation of what will happen if we do "X." Eventually we unravel the stimuli and substitute new ideas, interpretations, and meanings. These cue us that, although X happened, this activity, person, or situation is no longer dangerous and we are okay and free to move on.

Long-Term Solutions to Cyclical Fear

We can free ourselves from intrusive patterns of fear. We may never forget the event, and we may never be able to return to how we were before, but we don't have to fight the experience in our daily lives. We do not need to revisit the feelings regularly in order to heal them or keep ourselves safe. We can release the impact and choose to change thinking related to fear. As we become familiar with what sets off the cycle, we can interfere with those habitual responses and replace them with comfortable, rational, helpful responses.

MISCELLANEOUS FEARS

Deep Fears

Some fears can be buried deep within us. If the scary event happened early in life, say before we could talk, we may be hard pressed to understand a fear's origins. In cases of early abuse or catastrophe, clues about the original cause of the fear may be found later in life in our reactions to people, places, and situations as well as in what we avoid or in how we try to protect those we love.

There are several kinds of deep fears. *Suppressed fears* can be remembered without too much effort. A photograph, a piece of music, or certain kinds of questions can bring back these memories. *Repressed fears* are much tougher to get to. Repressed fears are blocked for good reasons. We need to proceed with caution when working with this type of deep fear because science and psychotherapy have not yet succeeded in being able to understand exactly how memory works.

Jennifer's Fear

Jennifer accused Howard, a neighbor, of abusing her four-year-old daughter. Howard had lived in the neighborhood for more than twenty years. During that time, no one else had made any accusations against Howard and his relationship with children. Jennifer said her daughter had told her that Howard had "done things to her." Later, in the course of the investigation, it became apparent that it was Jennifer who had been sexually abused by a neighbor at four, not her daughter. Jennifer had forgotten until her daughter turned the same age. This kind of deep-seated fear can have devastating consequences. Jennifer's fears were about herself, but it was only through acting on her fears about her daughter that Jennifer could "see" her past.

As the stories in this chapter illustrate, getting to the source of fear is not always straightforward. Fear shifts its shape. This helps each of us survive. Jennifer had to externalize the fear. She had to see it outside herself before she was able to find out what her own history had been. In other words, what originally was frightening often becomes part of an issue that must be solved through other means. The energy is there, but the energy does not easily get matched with the cause because it is too threatening. We seem to need to have it outside of us before we have that "Oh, that is about me" insight. This process is part of how our emotions find their way to the surface and tell us their stories.

Anxiety

Sometimes what was once a single fear has the potential to become, like dominoes, a *network* that is constantly and chronically on low alert. Some people experience a generalized free-floating anxiety that is attached to ever-expanding conscious and unconscious triggers. A cycle gets created in which the original fear and our responses expand. The first time we cycle through, we may include a smell, color, or sound as part of what causes a reaction. That new association may have had nothing to do with the original fear, but now, in our mind, it does. The layers of fear, our responses, and the new triggers may become panic or anxiety attacks.

One of the long-term results of this chronic hypervigilance is a weakening of the body's immune system. When our minds and our bodies are chronically "on call" and ready to take action or run away, our bodies continually manufacture adrenaline and the corresponding biochemical responses. This process, over time, can make us less able to deal with many situations because we are worn out. Or, we become afraid of so many stimuli that we cannot sort out our reactions.

The causes of anxiety may be difficult to unravel because the body's complex logic may not make sense to the person experiencing the anxiety. For example, a woman can no longer get to her job because she's become fearful of walking up stairs. This, in turn, causes more fear because she sees no connection between her fear of the stairs and some earlier event. Instead of blaming herself for yet another fear, the woman could first consider the new fear as a clue. She could consider that her body is trying to protect her, not cause her more harm. She is not being betrayed by her biochemistry. This may stop the spread of expanding responses. And then, with professional help, she can begin to back out of her fear, step-by-step.

In all likelihood, we may not be able to completely unravel our anxiety. Many of us can manage to unravel the most troubling anxiety on our own, through understanding the need for safety, releasing old memories, and creating new memories. But when the fear is overwhelming, the safest, easiest, fastest, and most effective way of resolving anxiety is with therapy, whether through cognitive-behavioral therapy, systematic desensitization, hypnosis, energy psychology, or a combination of methods. Professional therapists have many effective techniques for helping us lessen our fears.

Post-traumatic Stress Disorder

Like some forms of anxiety, post-traumatic stress disorder (PTSD) is a serious response to fear that is considered to be out of the self-help range and requires therapeutic intervention. This chapter includes PTSD because PTSD is prevalent and many don't know how to recognize or get help for it.

PTSD arises when a fear is so threatening that our system delays the actual experiencing of it until later. Our system goes into a kind of emotional shock. Situations in which our system throws this protective switch include war, abuse, murder, or torture.

When we are frozen or paralyzed by fear, we need expert help. A stopgap measure to employ until then is a hypnosis technique called *flooding*. Flooding involves choosing to crowd our thoughts with prepared images when we get the first inkling that a pattern of fear is imminent. Flooding helps us prepare for the pattern of fear by interrupting the usual process. Instead of being caught off guard without any options, we can practice what to do, whether focusing, phoning someone, praying, eating, doing a task that needs all our attention, or breathing into a small paper bag when hyperventilating. We can then seek professional help immediately.

This next example discusses PTSD as a result of sexual abuse, which is more common than we as a society may want to admit. For those who prefer not to read about sexual abuse, skip the next story.

Christine's Fear

Christine was six when her uncle moved into the house with her family. She was the second of three girls. Her uncle would always hug the girls and kiss them. Christine didn't like the smell of her uncle: stale and boozy was how she remembered it. But she knew her parents expected her to be polite to him.

At some point, the uncle began holding Christine on his lap, moving her around on him. She felt dirty afterward, but he always gave her a treat and told her it was their special secret. He also threatened to harm her sisters if she told anyone. This went on until he moved out two years later.

As an adult, Christine fell in love with a wonderful man but found sex with him almost repulsive. As she trusted him more and more, she began to feel increasingly aware of her reactions to him. Christine entered therapy with a sense that her distinctly nonsexual feelings were unfair to her husband. She described her reactions to being sexual with her husband as feeling frozen, not available. She found herself outside her body observing and making sure she was safe. These are common clues pointing to PTSD.

Christine's fears at the time of her uncle's abuse were too scary to feel. Some of her fears included

- not being a good daughter
- not being believed
- not trusting that her own feelings were legitimate
- ending her special relationship with her uncle, whom she loved, and causing herself to become less special
- causing something terrible to happen to her sisters

With all the contradictory emotions, how could a child bear to feel anything? Christine coped by avoiding her feelings. She shut off her body and her feelings and her mind. This was a great idea at the time. Doing so perhaps saved her life and helped her to survive to adulthood. But now, she wanted that frozen part back because her fears had become a liability.

Christine was courageous enough to let herself return to the point at which she had shut down. Through various techniques, she became able to re-experience, within her sessions, tremendous pent-up fears, sorrow, rage, and utter helplessness. Once she was able to name and acknowledge her experiences, the energy released. Physical release included tears, pounding, screaming, and shouting. She wanted to be whole in her marriage—no more pretending, no more avoiding. Eventually, Christine was able to have a more normal sexual relationship and move on in her life. Christine will always have her memories and a biochemical response, but because she has released so much of the fear, she now has more control over how she deals with her fears and has the means, awareness, desire, and safety to do so.

Therapists who work with memories must be careful and cautious with their clients about the process of remembering.

Through effective professional help, we may, over time, recognize reasons for our fears. We may be able to match the fear with the source and release the energy. And sometimes we discover that fear is only part of our story.

OTHER ASPECTS OF FEAR

Fear as an Emotional Ingredient

Fear often blends with other emotions to create more complex combinations. The table on pages 80 and 81 lists some combinations that include fear as one of the ingredients.

Combination	Threads of Fear
Surprise	Fear of not knowing what's going on. Surprises, by definition, are meant to "take someone un-awares." This can be pleasant or not, but regardless, we feel the fear.
Revulsion	Fear felt very physically due to some gut-level understanding. For example, we may see our food served by a waiter with dirty fin-gers and be afraid that our food is filthy and not fit to eat.
Anger	Fear can precede anger or vice versa, as when being bullied. We might feel the fear first, followed by anger that energizes us to want to act on the person bullying. Or we might feel anger toward the bully first but feel afraid to act on the anger due to the size or out-of-control behavior of the bully.
Shame	Fear that we have done some-thing to be ashamed of. Fear keeps the shamed person from fighting back, from getting to the bottom of the situation. Because shame is the result of another person's judgment or opinion, it is highly subjective. This means that the judgment or opinion is more about the person making it than about us. Often, the person

	doing the shaming is attempting to indirectly control us or get us to carry his or her emotions. If we take it on, we may find it paralyzing.
Jealousy	Fear that we cannot have something, do something, or be something. This fear can be a clue as to the true nature of our hopes, desires, and ambitions. By acknowledging what it is we want, we can then take action.
Sadness	Fear that love may be lost in some way, from loss of a job that we love to loss of a person whom we love.
Misunderstanding	Fear that others will not forgive mistakes or will hold us to a standard of perfection; fear of the judgment of others.

Fears That Become Projection and Prejudice

Fears not dealt with do not stay latent. Undischarged fear has energy associated with it and, therefore, thoughts associated with it. After being harmed by someone, we tend to feel more cautious; instinct instills a desire in us to avoid that "type" of person or situation. This makes sense physiologically and psychologically. For example, if a red-haired adolescent girl steals our purse, we will probably keep our eyes open when other red-haired girls come near us.

If we are not careful, we may begin to imagine or view this "type" through a lens of judgment. There are other options.

Instead of "projecting" our past experience onto innocent red-haired adolescents, we can take steps to protect ourselves. We buy a less accessible purse; we push ourselves to get to know other red-haired girls to balance out our prejudice; and we remember red-haired friends and family whose long track records with us have been nothing but loving. Then we let go.

There is always hope for greater freedom from the past. The body can detoxify from emotionally toxic events; cells can renegotiate what they do within the body; and the mind can be freed up to consider other ways of interpreting and responding to cues once the energy of the experience is released. The future is not written in stone.

FEAR EXERCISES

In these exercises, it is most important that you feel very safe. You will find an emotional inventory on pages 163–167. The questions will help release emotional energy for each fear and are especially useful in clearing away old emotional energy.

The exercises below are meant to help you specifically with fears that are more current. If you want to continue working with your emotional vocabulary, read over all the exercises here and start your day tomorrow with an awareness of your emotions either at home or at work. Continue to write in the notebook designated for learning about your emotions. Put your exercises in one place so you can see both your patterns and your solutions over time.

1. Keep track in your journal of when you feel fear, whether small fear or big, for the next two days. Note how you experience fear. What does your body do? Where do you feel fear? Does the fear move? What are your thoughts? Ask questions. What were the lights like?

What time of day was it? Describe everything you know from your senses. Your body can be a wealth of information. Instead of resisting body clues, try simply noticing them. *Be careful about how you interpret this information. Sometimes there has been no abuse. You do not know all the answers to why you seem to have certain reactions or thoughts, so be cautious.* For example:

I felt afraid about 4 P.M. in the afternoon, just as the sun was setting. I was walking to the bus stop. The air was cold and there were lots of people walking by. My attention was drawn to a woman who was standing near the bus stop. I glanced at her and noticed her very white face, but I also noticed her bright red lipstick. I felt afraid. I felt the fear first as a chill on the back of my neck and then as a desire to get as far away from her as possible, so I stood at the other end of the sidewalk. While I waited, I felt nervous in my stomach.

2. Try to be in relationship with fear. Jungian psychology suggests drawing as a safe way to connect with covert fear. Artwork can help. For example, you can use a mandala (a circle divided into four sections) to express on paper what is inside you. There are many books on mandalas, as well as community art courses.

3. Seek a support group or create one. Many communities have support groups specifically for fear-related issues. Some people start their own support groups. You can do so as well. You will want to ask a professional to help get you started. Sharing stories of success can be heartening to others. *However, be careful when sharing details of explicit situations, such as rape,*

sexual abuse, physical abuse, and other kinds of graphic details unless you have a professional therapist facilitating. Group members who are already scared may feel secondarily abused from hearing the details.

MOVING FORWARD

Fear, once experienced and released, can yield wisdom, growth, and myriad gifts, such as confidence, self-respect, strength, greater understanding, deeper faith, and ever more personal freedom.

As we let go, sometimes many times over, we keep focused on using the energy that fear makes available. We claim it, name it, reframe it, and then use it for our own purposes.

In the next chapter, we discover how gladness challenges us to create lives that invite satisfaction and contentment through practical internal means.

SIX

Gladness
Grace in Action

Gladness is the umbrella under which a variety of enjoyable feelings—from comfort to joy—fall. We are encouraged to experience and share this emotion. We have a near universal understanding that feeling good is an accepted goal and one to direct our lives toward. Becoming aware of what lies behind feeling glad empowers us to create the foundation for ongoing satisfaction and contentment. Being aware of the nuances and sources of this energy lets us structure our lives in ways that maximize the range and release of gladness.

The Gladness Continuum

tolerant	curious	pleased	excited	grateful	satisfied	happy	marvelous	peaceful	joyful

ABOUT GLADNESS

Feelings of gladness run the gamut. We may feel a general joy on holidays, in spiritual settings, or when we look at a puppy. We may feel happy when we are in love or when our team wins. As with the other emotions, gladness can be big or small, old or new, shared or not, and caused by something external or internal. We hear most about the big sources of gladness: a gift, prize, or accomplishment of a goal. We recognize this short-term excitement and happiness and want to share it. But gladness that is subtle and long-standing can be even more infectious and exciting.

THE ENERGY OF GLADNESS

We see the energy of gladness in curiosity, anticipation, and excitement. Whether we are rooting for our team, playing a game, enjoying a product, or feeling grateful for a helpful source, good doctor, dance instructor, hair stylist, book, movie, religion, or piece of music, we feel an energy that pushes us to share our information and enthusiasm with others. When a colleague comes to work on a Monday morning and tells a wonderful joke or story, the humor and enjoyment are contagious.

Gladness is very powerful. When we experience it, we want more of it. When our circumstances change and familiar sources of comfort, enrichment, and satisfaction disappear, we naturally don't want to lose access to what makes us happy. We may even try to block change. When we do this, we may end up resisting change that would ultimately create more wisdom, understanding, contentment, gratitude, and joy in our lives.

We live our lives based on believing that what we do will bring happiness, even if that means staying within a comfort zone that is unhealthy. Sometimes the more we force circumstances, the less happy we become.

The energy of gladness is a powerful motivator that lies at the base of many of our most important decisions.

THREE WAYS THAT GLADNESS ENTERS OUR LIVES

Good feelings come to us in three main ways: (1) on their own, (2) as a result of emotional ground we prepare without thinking, and (3) as a result of what we choose to practice and cultivate.

Joy	Joy comes to us unbidden, as in the grace of an important insight or intuition.
Peace	We prepare the ground for peace through how we live our lives.
Marvel	Marvel comes to us unbidden, as in a sunset that astonishes us.
Happiness	We prepare the ground for happiness by giving to others with a free and open heart.
Satisfaction (also contentment and comfort)	We can choose to set meaningful goals and move toward them.
Gratefulness	We prepare the ground for gratefulness through honesty and integrity. We can also choose to practice being grateful.
Excitement	We can choose to imagine, invest in, and focus on situations where ups and downs bring excitement, from sporting events to personal goals.
Pleasure	We can choose to give ourselves access to our senses and enjoy them.

Curiosity	We can choose to be curious, open, and in the moment.
Tolerance	We can choose to exercise understanding, patience, acceptance, and sharing.

Working through an emotional process leads to growing up and becoming mature, that is, dependable, responsible, and accountable for our actions and our lives. By letting the energy of emotions give us information about who we are, we receive the impetus to experience and even change our lives. It also helps us cultivate an interior life, made up of our experiences, beliefs, philosophies, theories, environments, and biology.

An Example: Going to Work While Looking for Another Job

Often we can create the groundwork for contentment, even when our environment or circumstances are not what we'd like. Looking for a new job while remaining in the one we want to leave creates a range of gladness possibilities.

We start with exercising tolerance for ourselves and our situation. Even though we may not like our job, we can prepare to enjoy the day. Before we go to work, we choose what snacks, music, clothes, interactions, and reinforcements we can give ourselves to boost our pleasure. We adjust our work environment: the air we breathe, the lighting, what we listen to, the clothes we wear, the food we eat, and the people we talk with and listen to. Obviously, we don't always have a choice in all areas, but we can boost the rate of pleasure in some ways.

We can give ourselves something to look forward to every day, whether it is before, during, or after work. We can insert a phone call into a coffee break, take a quick walk, write an e-mail to a friend, or keep a letter from or picture of someone who loves us close by.

We can choose to list all our reasons for being grateful: having a home to return to after work, a means to get to work, food, clothing, the job, our health, friends, family, and even our dissatisfaction that tells us to move on.

We can choose to be helpful to others at work. We can hold back a complaint or negative comment, avoid gossip, or do something that is helpful, such as opening a door or getting someone a cup of coffee.

By developing our curiosity, we can walk into the same old environment with a willingness to learn something new that day. We stop ourselves from regretting earlier decisions and putting off plans to enjoy ourselves after work. Instead, we spend our energy on finding what floats our spirit at work that day. We cultivate an attitude of openness until it's time to go home.

And, at the end of the day, we can walk to our car while getting drenched in rain. We can marvel at the sound of the rain and drive home satisfied, knowing that we invested in and contributed to our day. It is satisfying to know that we built something ourselves even if, to casual onlookers, nothing happened. We continue to lay the groundwork for contentment through our attitudes and actions.

BUILDING A FOUNDATION FOR GLADNESS

When we choose to exercise attitudes that invite possibility, we lay the foundation for peace and joy. The energetic qualities of peace and joy have no room for emotional static or anxiety, no need for looking beyond the moment, and no need to do more. In peace and joy, there is a kind of permission to just be, to accept and enjoy the flow of the moment that bathes us in the purest of energy. This brings us to a state of incredible emotional security and relaxation. This energy is stimulating, light, protective, and expansive, causing us to want nothing more.

Marriage is an example of how the cycle of gladness creates a firm foundation in our lives: it renews us and contributes to its renewal through our accountability, attitudes, and actions.

Tyrone and Marguerite's Marriage

Tyrone and Marguerite were married at what they considered to be the height of their lives. Both had jobs they liked, and they were very much in love. They described their wedding day as "walking on air lovestruck." About six months after the honeymoon, the economy changed. Tyrone lost his job at about the same time that Marguerite became pregnant. There were arguments, accusations, and doubts about the strength of their marriage. But when they got beyond the new fears that had entered their lives, they realized that each of them was doing his or her best; each of them was being honest and responsible. At that point, they were able to establish a foundation of trust and mutuality that created contentment and even joy.

Through learning to take responsibility for their own actions and emotions, they were able to keep the new marriage from bearing the burden of all their difficulties. They used their emotions to build a strong base that supported their marriage. Throughout the difficulties, and after their baby was born, joy cycled through their lives. The magic of love and joy are results of qualities inside of us, not outside of us. The world does not need to go our way in order to have joy.

Some of us expect a foundation to be there because we are married. The foundation is not a given. It is the result of holding on to integrity, sharing information, communicating, and taking risks.

There is an ease to a relationship when trust has had time to grow, when doubts have been worked through, and when we know in our hearts that the other person is giving his or her utmost to the marriage. We can encourage peace and contentment through communication, through not taking one another for granted, and through being respectful even in the midst of a heated discussion. The safety and trust created by each person's willingness then grows and contributes to a sense of well-being and contentment, so that even when there are other problems, the gears of the relationship are not grinding.

Establishing a footing built on trust (a kind of personal peace between two people), gratitude (for the gift of love from another, as well as the gift of being able to love another), and respect (the honoring of another) contributes to gladness in a relationship. When the fire of passion or joy is not at the forefront, these solid qualities can carry relationships for very long periods.

INTERNAL VERSUS EXTERNAL SOURCES OF GLADNESS

Gladness and its varieties come from *internal* and *external* sources. *Internal* sources result in feelings that become part of us and can be drawn on as wisdom and self-knowledge. For example, Kim wants to be a swimmer. She takes lessons. She begins competing. She puts in long hours to build strength, strategy, and understanding. She comes in third in a competition. She feels great! Not only has Kim's swimming brought her to a goal, but the process of getting there has brought her self-confidence because she has discipline (the ability to stay with something) and self-respect (she took risks, faced fears, and won). This *internal* process has developed many strong character traits in Kim. Discipline and self-respect contribute to Kim's long-term gladness.

External sources of gladness are often easier to access because they involve material things. But the gladness acquired from most externals usually does not last very long, is less meaningful, and is less likely to contribute to self-knowledge or wisdom. For example, Jeff is small for his age. He feels helpless when other kids make fun of him at his middle school. His parents don't understand how helpless he feels. They don't know how to "fix" it. So, they give him a DVD player and DVDs. Now he can watch movies in his room when he gets home from school. Jeff loves the movies. But when they are over, he does not feel more self-respect, self-confidence, or self-sufficiency.

This is not to say that external means do not help us grow or satisfy us to a certain degree. Purchasing a high-quality camera can lead us to a fulfilling career in photography. Owning a dependable car can get us to a fulfilling job every day. It is when we depend on material things or expect them to bring us happiness that we get into trouble. Having the best stereo system in the neighborhood may give us a good feeling for a week or so, but as time wears on, we feel an emptiness where the gladness once was. We cannot sustain the feeling for long.

If we do not realize that internal sources are important ingredients for happiness and that we are co-creators of the conditions for happiness, we may begin to panic when the good feelings run dry. If our belief is that happiness depends on external things, events, or people, we might start buying more or investing more in relationships to chase that "good" feeling. The belief that doing more or getting more equals more satisfaction may cause us to drift even farther away from the real thing.

It is important not to judge our feelings. What we think makes us feel good is not always good for us, and what we think makes us feel bad is not necessarily bad for us. For example, drug use can lead to death while losing a job may lead us to more rewarding work.

WHEN WE ARE UNAWARE OF
INTERNAL SOURCES OF GLADNESS

Many of us think that we have little to do with internal sources of satisfaction. We do not know or believe that we are capable of tapping into these sources. We may think that people either have these sources or they don't. If we don't know how to access our internal sources of gladness, we feel compelled to look at external sources. Why wouldn't we? Our culture overwhelmingly supports this idea of external comforts by continually generating products that are guaranteed to make us "happier" or "better" people.

For some of us, the external source may be something that we take internally, such as food or drugs; that we acquire through a process, such as through gambling or having sex; or that we possess, such as clothes or cars. We may feel superior to other people if we own the perfect home, tend the biggest garden, or have the best job. We may attempt to control or outdo others or make sure we win at all costs. These external sources of gladness eventually sour. Once we "win," where do we next set our sights? Pursuing "highs" like these can drive us into unhealthy patterns.

Externals give us a hint of the real thing. When that hint is mistaken for the final goal, then we've settled for too little. People who hit bottom in addictions, from gambling to drugs, are forced to face their belief system about where sources of gladness are located. Hitting bottom may finally outweigh the delusions. Facing the fact that the external search does not lead to satisfaction or contentment can be terrifying. Our beliefs that support only external methods of contentment, however, can be changed, expanded, overridden, or deleted.

Daniel's Story

Daniel had been a shy adolescent. He began to drink at age twelve. At that age, he chose to shut out his inner self. In fact, he hated and was scared of himself, of what might exist inside him. When he sobered up at twenty-three, he was nearly out of his mind with terror. Daniel had given up his means for feeling better and controlling his life, and now he felt empty, immature, and scared. Sobering up created a serious emotional and spiritual emergency. Daniel did not believe he had the tools to stay sober or make a life for himself without alcohol.

One of the many turning points in Daniel's recovery happened in group therapy. Daniel was the focus of the group's feedback. His peers told him they liked his sense of humor, and they gave him specifics about how funny he is. This was the first of many events that gave Daniel the hope he needed to face himself. He needs a lot of support and probably always will, but he has gone from eating out of garbage cans to holding a job and living in a subsidized apartment. He brings smiles to other people, and his brave willingness to face himself and grow an interior life has been a lifeline for others.

We can find the means to shed light onto the garden that is our interior world. We plant the seeds that eventually nourish our desires and dreams. And we let others care about us, as well.

In giving up the belief that we are in charge of creating gladness by buying it, securing it, or hoarding it, we lose our insulation and begin to open to other possibilities, people, spirit, and inspiration. People who do this find that many enjoyable aspects of living return. By creating conditions that enhance the potential for gladness, we find other qualities that enrich our lives, such as gratitude, comfort, and contentment. These emotional qualities create a foundation that will sustain us when we face difficulties.

Many aspects of gladness are available through our own efforts. We practice, we try new things no matter how old we get; we follow our dreams and intuitions; we experiment with interests, hobbies, with communicating; and we learn from our many mistakes.

QUICK FIXES CAN BECOME HABITUAL

Sometimes, even when we know what to do, we don't have the energy or time to cultivate gladness. So we look for a "quick fix." We choose what is within our grasp, convenient, and under our control.

Sometimes the quick fix does the trick, like buying a CD or talking with a friend. But we need to do this judiciously because when the desire to avoid an issue becomes habit, the problem seems to collect an energy of its own. When we don't develop emotional tools or support, when we put off life's problems, or when we don't value and seek resolution of the issues, our chronic neglect of ourselves can undo us.

Growing through life experiences is cumulative. The more we *face* obstacles, the more comfort, satisfaction, and gladness we secure and the less vulnerable we are to outside intrusions. Our growth determines how our lives will unfold.

Dale's Story

Dale wanted to be a writer and identified himself as such. Dale had not taken classes or had any training, but he loved the idea of being a playwright. He thought saying he was a playwright was the same as working through the process of becoming a playwright. He wanted the status he believed would be conferred on him. He associated with writers. They often gave him ideas and helped him with rewrites. Dale worked hard on his image through marketing and public relations. He sent articles he had written about himself to the paper and made friends with those who could take his picture or give him favorable reviews.

However, Dale's interaction with other writers was not mutual. Dale did not want to hear about their success. The need for interior security and gratification grew as Dale used up his external means. Dale neither earned nor received respect from tolerant colleagues. His image fooled some people, but for those who knew him, Dale was considered selfish and negative.

Dale's impulse to create, while wonderful, was misused. Instead of allowing art to shape and change him, he took the easy way out. He grabbed at the goodies of creativity, instead of allowing them to evolve out of his work. Dale did not cultivate a situation that could bring satisfaction. He avoided responsibility for facing his emptiness by faking an image and trying to seduce others with it.

Dale's plan eventually backfired. Once the plays were over and the audience gone, Dale was left with his emptiness. Dale had done just about everything but the work of facing self-doubt, taking risks that meant something to him, and learning about the willingness to change. Dale was living a lie.

When we do not tend to our interior lives or when we misuse our interior lives, we are left with emptiness. Instead of regarding this emptiness as a call to live, investigate, and discover, we sometimes choose to run, balk, or play games with our-selves. But this emptiness can be filled with riches beyond be-lief. As we mature and evolve, we can reap results that are impressively satisfying. Our experiences give us something re-fined and meaningful to offer others. We are no longer threat-ened by others' success. We garner tremendous freedom by having a familiar, dependable emotional reserve to draw from. And sometimes, when there is a groundswell of satisfaction, contentment, and gratitude, our gladness becomes joy.

GLADNESS AND JOY

Joy is a special outburst of incredibly positive energy that may build to the point of a peak experience called ecstasy. For many of us, this category of joy is a result of our spiritual beliefs, prac-tices, and relationship with self, others, and a God of our under-standing. This joy is possible through meditation, prayer, and, sometimes, the support of a religious or spiritual group. Joy of this nature is often associated with compassion, generosity, and unconditional love. Saints, gurus, clerics, and holy people throughout the ages have shared their methods for finding this joy.

These enlightened people believe that spiritual joy is our birthright and that all people have equal access to this state of being. We need to seek it within. This joy can inform everything we do throughout our lives. It is a powerful source of guidance, support, and contentment.

GLADNESS AND GRACE

A friend recently brought up the topic of grace, or what might also be known as a benevolent free-of-charge gift from out of nowhere. His question to me was "When you look back at your life, how many times did you *refuse* grace?" I found this question intriguing because the element of grace comes in so many forms without announcement. By asking the question in this way, he defined grace as the goodness that comes to us from friends, strangers, coincidences, or other means. When he used the term "grace" instead of "offers for help," "information," or "time offered by others," he shifted the meaning and source of the goodness.

Sometimes grace is made obvious by the person offering it. Sometimes grace is so subtle that we may not even recognize it, such as taking our food, homes, employment, and loved ones for granted. Grace may come through a person, a friend, a stranger, a domestic or wild animal, a word, a smile, or a mysterious connection. It may appear in a musical phrase, a chore, or a seeming obstacle. One such concrete example for me came when I was driving through Pennsylvania at night. I was driving a small car. It was raining. I was driving through the mountains alone on a four-lane highway. All of a sudden, I heard a voice inside my head. "Get in the other lane," it commanded. I did so immediately, even though there were no other vehicles in sight. Within seconds, I passed a dead deer lying in my previous lane. I was moved by this unknown grace and have continued to reflect on its mystery with gratitude.

But not all grace needs to be so dramatic. When a friend offers support or a kind word, when someone calls us asking for forgiveness and we give it, when someone we have hurt forgives us, when someone notices us in a positive way and mentions it—these are all free gifts. Have we turned them away? Have we been too busy to notice the free beauty around us? Have we refused to change when grace showed up in the form of concern?

There are no guarantees for any of us. But in noticing and acknowledging grace, we increase the range of our emotions in an easy, nonthreatening way.

When we share our gladness with others, we share a positive energy that will also remind them of their gladness. We will have fewer regrets later about whether we hid our lights under a basket or whether our loved ones knew how much we needed, loved, and respected them. To live fully is to feel fully—and that includes pleasure, contentment, happiness, and utter joy.

GLADNESS EXERCISES

You will find an emotional inventory on pages 163–167. The questions will help you become more aware of what has made you glad and why over the years. The exercises that follow here will help you become aware of what currently contributes to the range of your good feelings. They will also help you build an even stronger foundation for self-confidence and gratitude. They are good for jump-starting negative moods, as well as for learning what sets the stage for contentment.

If you want to continue working with your emotional vocabulary, read over all the exercises here and start on them today. Continue to write in the notebook designated for learning about your emotions. Put your exercises in one place so you can see both your patterns and your solutions over time.

1. Call a friend and share a good moment from today. Ask what he or she is grateful for.
2. Look in your closet this week and notice the clothing you have come to enjoy wearing. Write down what you appreciate in your wardrobe, including those people or that job that has contributed to your having these belongings.
3. Look at one person or pet in your household and notice everything you love about him or her. Write down the specifics in your notebook.

4. When you have a few quiet moments, make a gratitude list. List at least ten things you are grateful for today.

5. Make three columns on a piece of paper. In the first column, make a list of the free gifts that you've been given. In the second column, note whether the gifts came in the form of love, concern, care, feedback, requests, questions, objects, suggestions, support, or incidents. In the third column, list whether you accepted or rejected the gifts and your reasons. Note the emotions associated with refusing or accepting. Look for patterns. Decide whether to make changes in learning how to accept more and let go of the results. For example:

Free Gifts	Form	Accepted or Refused, and Why
A phone call from a friend	Love	Accepted it because I love the company of my friends
A compliment from my supervisor	Feedback	Refused it because I am afraid he'll expect more if I accept

6. On another piece of paper, make three columns. In the first, list those who have helped you and what they did. In the second column, list major accomplishments you believe you have achieved by yourself. Give the list to a spouse, child, close friend, or relative and ask that person to describe what he or she remembers about your achievements. Write their responses in the third column. Talk about the results.

Those Who Have Helped Me	What I Have Done on My Own	What Others Remember about My Achievements
I am grateful to my father for teaching me to love music, the outdoors, reading, and how to have fun.	I got myself a job at a major corporation.	My brother knew someone who worked at the corporation, and he helped me get the interview.
I am grateful to my mother for teaching me to be gentle, sensitive, kind, and generous.	I won the swimming event at the state competition.	My father took me to lessons and paid for them. He went to every meet.

MOVING FORWARD

Sometimes we can get so wrapped up in ourselves that we think we've created all the gladness in our lives. It can be a joy to realize how much we've been loved and helped by others.

The next chapter describes what makes sorrow so complicated.

SEVEN

Sorrow

A Complicated Accumulation

Sorrow, or sadness, is the emotion at the crux of a loss cycle. We spend our lives being passionate about and invested in people, situations, ideas, philosophies, and other engaging and intriguing interests. At the beginning of our love affair with people, pets, jobs, or ideas, we don't spend a lot of time considering what may happen if or when we lose them. While knowing full well that everything on the planet, human and otherwise, is not permanent, we give ourselves over to our passions. Building a relationship is a process, but so is losing a relationship. The cycle of sadness takes us through the many layers of what a specific person or idea means to us. In understanding the meaning, we know the depth of our sadness.

This chapter covers the energy of sadness and gives us ways to release some of the feelings that go along with it.

The Sorrow Continuum

disappointed blue hurt distressed pained tearful desolate grief-stricken hopeless

ABOUT SORROW

Sorrow may be old or new, big or small, fleeting or long-standing. Sorrow's energy feels denser and heavier than that of other emotions. Sorrow requires that we make time for it—to feel sad, to cry, to miss what we have lost, to feel the love that is no longer returned—so it is the easiest emotion to postpone.

THE ENERGY OF SORROW

The energy of sorrow, while subtle, can quietly accumulate. If we neglect this energy, we may find ourselves crying "over nothing" or feeling threatened by overwhelming sadness when we least expect it. We may begin to fear being sad: What if we let go? What if the tears start? What if we can't stop crying?

Feeling sorrow, grieving, mourning, and shedding tears cleanse and release pent-up emotions. Shedding tears opens up places for new understandings to unfold. Crying helps us grow up. When we make time and devote energy, attention, and love to a person or pet after he or she leaves us, we are acknowledging not only his or her value but also our own. We are noting the risks, the love, the commitment, and all that goes along with deep involvement. We begin to realize how following our sorrow to its core helps us value our capacity to love and acknowledge how much this special person or pet meant and will continue to mean to us.

TYPES OF SORROW

As we look at the sorrow continuum, we notice that all the aspects of sorrow can be big or small, as in being very disappointed because we did not reach an important goal or a little disappointed because we lost a favorite pen.

The sad energy generated by a small loss is fairly easy to disperse. If we lose a favorite pen, we ask ourselves questions: "Where did I last see it?" "Where did I last use it?" We ask other people, "Have you seen my pen?" And we look for the pen. At some point, if we don't find it, we give up. Maybe we feel a bit sad because it was a special pen. We then turn our attention toward getting another pen, and that particular disappointment is pretty much resolved.

When the disappointment is more involved because we invested more time, energy, care, and meaning into the process, we find the energy of sorrow harder to shed. For example, the Antonellises want very much to adopt a child from a certain country. They went through the adoption process, did the homework, and were approved. Now, their hopes, dreams, and imaginations fill in the blanks about what the child and their family will be like. If the government in that country changes its adoption standards and suddenly forbids adoptions, the Antonellises suffer huge disappointment. Their loss is emotional, social, spiritual, intellectual, cultural, and financial—substantial losses that affect them deeply. The healing process includes not only feeling sad about the loss of these particular dreams but also needing to detach from original dreams and replace them with new expectations. The dreams don't die, but the specifics must change. That takes a willingness to risk disappointment again.

The following table lists each point along the sorrow continuum. Each is described and then followed by a possible outcome if the emotion is acknowledged, felt, and released.

Disappointed	We or something we're invested in falls short of our hopes and dreams. As a result, we may feel unfulfilled, unsuccessful, disillusioned, and frustrated. (Work through to hope.)
Blue	If we don't take care of our sadness after a painful experience,

	we may feel dispirited, dejected, and downhearted. (Work through to cheerfulness.)
Hurt	This sadness relates to physical and emotional wounds, as in being offended or bruised. (Work through to pleasure.)
Distressed	When we are lacking comfort or the basics in our physical, emotional, and spiritual lives—such as food, friendship, and help—we are sad in an ongoing, troubled way. (Work through to safety.)
Pained	When we have been victimized, intentionally or not, we may ache physically and emotionally. (Work through to comfort.)
Tearful	When we lose something, especially when our loss is that of someone we love, we feel tearful and our outlook tends toward being heavy-hearted, unhappy, dismal, and gloomy. (Work through to optimism.)
Desolate	Accumulated disappointments such as emotional, physical, spiritual, financial, social, and cultural losses can bring us to our knees. We see the world as bleak and inhospitable, and we feel we have been abandoned and forgotten. (Work through to being sociable.)

Grief-stricken	Sudden sadness, such as the loss of someone with whom we have unfinished business, may cause poignant suffering that can incapacitate us. (Work through to being at ease.)
Hopeless	When our tools for releasing emotions are limited but our expectations about being capable of dealing with life are high, unexpected losses can shock us into feelings of desperation, despondency, and pessimism that, if turned inward, can lead to suicide. (Work through to hope and expectancy.)

HOW MUCH ARE WE BEING AFFECTED?

There are many aspects of sorrow that contribute to how much we are affected. For example, sorrow may be based in externals (*how* we are being treated) and internals (*what* are our expectations), as well as whether the sorrow is large or small, new or old.

Sorrow can also combine with other emotions. For example, a moment of disappointment may contain the emotional ingredients of sorrow, anger, and fear. If we lose a good umbrella, we are sad to have lost it, angry that we weren't careful, and fearful that we won't find a good replacement. In this case, the energy of sorrow seems to lift off easily because the problem has an easy solution. We can buy another umbrella and the sorrow, for the most part, is released. If the lost object were a ring that a relative had given us years ago and was of great sentimental value, then there is no solution. The sadness is much greater because no matter how many other rings we acquire, we won't have that one.

When very important sorrows have no solution, as is often the case, we find the energy of sorrow cycling periodically through our lives. Sometimes we find ourselves remembering experiences that seem to come out of nowhere. Other times, we realize that an anniversary date, birthday, holiday, or experience revives our sadness. Each time we find ourselves back in the cycle of remembering and feeling sad, we can release what sorrow we are able to access. The sorrow exercises at the end of this chapter suggest ways to excavate sorrow and use it to support our emotional lives.

If a loss is important to you, shedding tears once will probably not be enough. Alan's story explains why.

Alan's Grief

Alan's mother died when he was eleven. He began grieving when he was eleven. When he turned twelve, he grew in his understanding of the world and the meaningfulness of his mother's love for him and the way she enriched his life. While he was twelve, Alan's grief included this new understanding. At twenty, when he married and his mother was not there to see his new bride or advise him about having children, he began a new grief cycle—for all that did not and would not happen in terms of his marriage. Alan had to get through another layer of self-understanding in this cycle of loss. When Alan's children are born, he will again expand his understanding of what has been lost. He will be aware that his children will not enjoy the richness that his mother could have added to their lives. Alan will not have the opportunity to watch his mother and children form a relationship.

Alan's sorrow is not necessarily a daily occurrence, but when it comes—on anniversaries, birthdays, holidays, special times, or out of the blue—he lets himself feel it. He tells his wife, he calls his father, he writes to his sister, or he puts it in a letter to a childhood friend who knew his mother. Alan's loss is cyclical, deep, layered, ongoing, and sometimes expanding.

A major loss, such as the loss of a parent or a child, generates an intense and complex energy. And small wonder. Where do we put all the love we have for that person? All the complexity of good and bad times, all the words said and regretted, love left unsaid, feelings left unexpressed, vulnerabilities left hidden, lies told for good and bad reasons, and the finality of death combine to make the loss of a loved one incredibly difficult. All the unmet expectations, the hurts, the joys, the fears, and, for many, the day-to-day pain of watching a loved one become ill and gradually succumb is shattering. Much that has been swept under the rug for a lifetime gets resurrected. Energy, loving and sorrowful, fearful and angry, returns—sometimes slowly and sometimes quickly with unexpected force. This energy becomes part of the cycle, and as we allow memory, love, meaning, and loss to cycle through, we grieve. Many of us will do this throughout our lives.

THE IMPORTANCE OF CLOSURE

We hear about people wanting *closure* when those they love die. Closure is both external and internal. We may want estates settled, lawsuits brought and concluded, or criminals imprisoned. Once these kinds of external issues are resolved, we can release the focus on injustice, putting closure to external sorrow.

But closure does not apply to emotions. We don't get closure on internal sorrow, even though we may want it. We may get closure on accepting that the person we love is gone. We may get closure on some angry feelings if we accept death and its many ramifications. But sorrow is lifelong. Only the phases of sorrow moderate and change over time.

THE COURSE OF SORROW

Each of us goes through the course of sorrow differently. For all of us, social expectations can be brutally insensitive when the outside world considers us weak, depressed, childish, not "bucking up," or not "getting on with it." Often when we lose a loved one, we are expected to return to work within two weeks, perhaps talk about the loss for a week or two, and then move on.

Because we are the one going through the pain, we alone know how much this person, pet, project, or idea means to us. We have very specific ways of going toward healing, which can be supported and smoothed for us by others. Those helping us do not determine whether we have cried enough or spent enough time on what has happened. Those who want to stanch our sorrow often have no idea when they are doing it for themselves, not for us. It is so hard for them to witness our pain. They feel helpless, and in many ways, they are. They want us to stop so their own sorrows aren't triggered. They may reach out a hand and say, "Please don't cry. Let's go do something."

Feeling sad requires that we relax, wait patiently as we would for a friend, open up, and do our best to welcome however sadness appears. Sorrow often asks us to wait, to become quiet, so that we can connect our memories with what is missing. Instead of taking action, we have to give in and allow the sorrow to find its way through us. We need to make ourselves vulnerable.

LETTING SORROW FIND ITS WAY

Time and space are needed to help us quiet down and feel sorrow. This *inaction* helps sorrow find its way in us. Friends can help by simply listening and providing ears, eyes, and a willingness to witness whatever comes out. The *action* comes when we are quiet enough to explore those places of hurt where our memories are raw and the emotions are ready to release. We neither force the feelings nor hold them back. The emotions release as we sit with the discomfort and restlessness that precede the tears.

Sometimes we act on the restlessness and thereby postpone our sorrow. The restlessness can be so intense that we keep busy, filling our lives with objects, work, and problems. Taking our mind off our troubles is often a good idea, but when grief asks to be attended to, the best action is often simply to "be" until the tears stop naturally.

We need to exercise caution about using prescription drugs during times of grief.

Surrendering to sorrow and being supported in that surrender releases the energy and also clears space for our day-to-day interactions. But when we numb the feelings, ignore them, create drama as a substitution, or harm ourselves, we invite a general dulling of all our emotions, which can become depression.

Anger can feel more powerful than sorrow and it is a step in the process of grieving a loss, but we must eventually get to the sorrow. If we don't, then as we try to release the energy of sorrow, we may create a pattern of drama by picking arguments with friends and family, showing up late to work until we're fired, getting into accidents, or ending relationships with others so they'll be in pain. Energy gets released but not clearly, cleanly, or for the long term. Provoking anger in others will not release our anger or sorrow.

Kathie's Unfinished Business
Sometimes closure has to do with needing to finish our business with another. For example, Kathie's mother was

killed in a car accident. The night before the accident, Kathie had argued with her mother about money that her mother owed her. The conversation ended badly. Kathie loves her mother and is grief-stricken over her mother's sudden death. Kathie will have to deal with not only the sorrow that goes with the end of her long-standing relationship but also the nature of her conversation with her mother the night before she died. This is called unfinished business. Unfinished conversations and incomplete understandings can cause lifelong sorrow. Closure for Kathie may include having a one-sided conversation with her mother. Even though her mother is no longer living, Kathie, whether in a letter or through verbalizing with a friend or counselor, can write or say what she most wants her mother to know, hear, and understand. Doing this will help her release some of the energy.

An interesting aspect of sorrow is that it may persist even when it involves something or someone who harmed us. People who have been sexually abused often hate their perpetrators, are very angry with them, and yet may miss them. Victims may miss their perpetrators for the same reasons all of us miss others: for the attention, for any good times or moments that came out of that relationship, or for forming our lives by teaching us.

WHAT TO DO WHEN FEELINGS ARE INTENSE

Sorrow can be intense at times, and it is important to know when we need help with it. If the sadness becomes overwhelming, we may begin to numb out or seek chemical substitutions instead of crying. We may look for a new relationship to fill the void instead of sitting with the emptiness and giving ourselves time to heal. We may work too much and stay too tired to think. We may avoid people, places, and situations in which the subject of our sorrow might come up. We may neglect spiritual support. We may become less and less able to deal with any emotions associated with loss. And sometimes when we feel powerlessness over ourselves, we try wielding power over others. We may become verbally, physically, or sexually abusive. Or we may become destructive toward ourselves by failing to eat, eating too much, cutting ourselves, overdoing alcohol, and so forth. These clues point to our tremendous needs for comfort, safety, support, and help with loss.

Through getting help from a clergyperson, counselor, or friend, we can contain the amount of time we spend considering and feeling sorrow. And we can release pieces of the sadness in safety. Most of us need help in going through the loss of loved ones. Many support groups offer help with sadness of all types, including support for loss through cancer, addiction, crime, or mental illness. Many of these groups are free. They are usually listed in the phone book under social agencies or in the newspaper under community meetings.

LOSING OUR ILLUSIONS

Sometimes, losing our illusions can be more painful than the actual loss, especially when it comes to our illusions relating to other people.

When I was in my twenties, I fell for a man who seemed familiar to me. He felt like family even before I knew him well. His glasses reminded me of those worn by my mother, who had passed away. His cigarette smoking reminded me of both my parents. His way of sitting quietly reminded me of my mother. His height reminded me of my father. In many ways, he was a visceral and physical reminder of my parents. Unfortunately for me, his quietness was not of peace but of nicotine-soaked numbness. When he gave up smoking, he also gave up the quietness and became a poor match for me. He was not the person I had *imagined*.

In my mind and heart, I had concocted him to be a sensitive person like my mother. Suddenly, I saw through my own needy projection to a person not at all like my mother. I saw someone philosophically, ethically, emotionally, spiritually, and intellectually very unlike my mother or anyone else I would want to share my life with.

I saw the handwriting on the wall and knew I would have to move on, but I was concerned with how much pain I was going to feel. I knew that because I had projected good family feelings onto this person, I would have to take the projections back. I had to let go of loving my family through him. I had to let go of my illusions that were bound up with love for my mother and father. I had already lost my mother, whom I loved very much. Now I had to lose the illusion of her as well.

When my relationship with this man ended, I was overtaken by waves of grief. I wasn't missing him; I was missing my mother all over again. I was feeling leftover grief that I had not acknowledged until this circumstance reminded me. I knew I didn't have deep feelings for this man, but I felt very connected to him. Once it ended, I saw that the depth of my emotions were not much related to the here and now. This acknowledgment felt like an old iceberg breaking free and cruising at breakneck speed to dissolution. The ensuing tears released some old ties that I had to my mother.

After that episode, I seemed to have healed an important wound. I did not need to use projection as a substitute for real relationships. I met a man with whom I fell deeply in love, and I am now happily married to that wonderful person.

On the sorrow continuum, I was grief-stricken over the loss of my mother. If I had not given myself over to those tears when the opportunity arose, I might still be repeating that history.

AVOIDING SORROW

Not feeling sorrow invites fear into our lives. The longer we put off feeling sorrow, the greater our fear of it becomes. Postponing the expression of that sorrow causes its energy to grow. The interesting thing is that we may eventually lose track of what we have lost, as well as the grief. Over time, sorrow may be replaced by anger or fear. When we start to get quiet and sorrow begins to well up, we become angry. We don't want to deal with pain. We are angry that we lost someone we love. We are afraid of feeling vulnerable. When these other emotions cover up the original emotion of sorrow, we can't unravel the puzzle. To heal pain, we need to feel it. To feel it, we need to name it.

Jamal's Story

Jamal was in his thirties and had not cried since high school, even when his classmate and best friend had died of leukemia his senior year. In his twenties, Jamal was not about to give in to what he regarded as weakness. He became a good salesman, and his love of selling served him well. Over time, though, he began to have panic attacks that left him feeling helpless and very angry, mostly with himself, which is when he came to see me.

In the course of his counseling, Jamal tried to give me reasons instead of feelings. He fought feeling. He tried to sell me on his reasons for the panic attacks. He did not want to feel anything. Jamal really struggled with many of my suggestions for releasing his sorrow, but the day I saw tears in his eyes was the beginning of his real control. As he was able, slowly and safely, to experience small bits of sadness, he began to develop a relationship with himself— one that he had never had before. He began to trust that he could feel sorrow without losing his mind and without being ridiculed. In time, Jamal's panic gave way to a more balanced emotional response. As his trust in himself grew, he felt confident that he could live with his emotions, including sorrow.

Jamal created self-alienation by keeping his feelings at bay and lying about how he was affected by life, which led to an interior conflict. Just as we might teach a friend that we aren't trustworthy by lying to him or her, Jamal created a lack of trust in himself when he did not take care of his emotional business.

SORROW AS BACKGROUND

Low-grade sorrow is an emotion that often stays in the background. There are many occasions in our lives, from the moment we are born, to experience loss. Some of us are very sensitive to loss, and others have many losses. For example, external forces can contribute to a sense of loss, as when children go hungry, an ethnic group is scapegoated, or parents are ill or addicted. These losses may become chronic and lurk in the background. Pain and sorrow caused by environmental factors are devastating, and for some, these sorrows become a normal state.

For example, infants are well equipped to let caretakers know when they need something. Their crying has a jagged edge that implies how very important their needs are. When infants are ignored, they may learn that crying is meaningless. In this way, their feelings of helplessness can lead to chronic sorrow. If feeling sad is what feels normal, we may seek out those who will reinforce our sadness, such as people who ignore us. Or we may find situations that allow us to repeat painful experiences. Sadness becomes as natural as breathing. It is where we feel comfortable.

Even those of us who come from safe and supportive families have a background sorrow that comes from understanding what it means to be human. At some point, we realize that each day, when it is over, will not be lived again, no matter how beautiful. Each breath, once exhaled, will not come again. This *existential* sorrow differs from other sorrows. There is no way to avoid it. But acknowledging existential sorrow may spur us to find meaningful, healthy lives. We may find work, relationships, or spiritual connections that bridge our fears. Living with paradoxical emotions—sorrow and gladness—can enhance our ability to accept each day as a gift. In remembering how vulnerable we are, in incorporating the energy of this background sorrow, we can derive even more satisfaction from the challenge of growing interior and exterior lives.

Dr. Therese Rando, in her wonderful and comprehensive book *Treatment of Complicated Mourning,* makes it clear that life is not just a series of separate events. Each grief event is tied in a process to other grief events that happened before and may well happen again. Each grief is a building block, either to be dismantled or not. If we don't let go of our grief, we build walls around our heart and thoughts until we shut out life, including its healing possibilities.

RELEASING SORROW

We can prepare ourselves to feel sorrow by acknowledging that it is a universal emotion. Each of us will experience the sadness of loss. We may not always choose which losses will come into our lives, but by involving ourselves in smaller losses as they come along, we can form a relationship with ourselves about loss. We can develop tools for dealing with loss.

SORROW EXERCISES

These exercises can help you resurrect old sorrow or connect to current sorrow. You can use the emotional inventory on pages 163–167 for help with general and old sorrow.

The exercises that follow here will help you become aware of current sorrow and help you release some of it. They may not bring up the sadness right away, but they may increase your awareness. Then, when the feelings need expression, you can welcome them instead of resisting.

If you want to continue working with your emotional vocabulary, read over all the exercises here and start on them today. Continue to write in the notebook designated for learning about your emotions. Put your exercises in one place so you can see both your patterns and your solutions over time.

1. Keep a journal for two days. Note any time when you feel sad, whether it is the result of the news, something visual, something personal, or listening to music.

2. Give yourself permission to create a safe haven for your sorrow and tears: a quiet afternoon or several hours of free time without interruptions. You may want to use a candle or incense, music that soothes or helps, clothing that comforts, or even a picture from your past.

3. List losses you may have caused yourself, such as marrying the wrong person knowingly or denying yourself the career you really want. Take the time to admit these things to yourself. Note what the losses

and the results have been. Then write yourself a letter apologizing for your errors.

4. List times you have harmed others or they have harmed you. Write a letter asking for forgiveness. You can ask forgiveness from your spiritual source, from the person(s) you harmed, and from yourself. Sometimes having the *willingness* to write the letter will illuminate what is not clear. That may be enough. Often, the feelings that come with offering forgiveness or receiving forgiveness are the missing pieces needed for healing.

Before you send a letter asking for forgiveness, check with a friend or mentor about the safety of doing so. For example, if you feel you reacted badly to another's verbal abuse, in asking for forgiveness, you may give the abuser permission to think that he or she was right in having abused you. Writing the letter is one action. Sending it is entirely another. You do not have to send the letter in order to effect healing.

---

5. Give yourself permission to cry as many tears as necessary. You will not be crying the same tears over and over. You are crying, cleansing, and releasing for particular events, and eventually, the sorrow and heaviness will lift and disperse.

6. If you are sad and don't know why, then simply allow the sadness. Many of us need to cry throughout our lives without necessarily knowing the reasons. This release of pain is important and cleansing.

MOVING FORWARD

Sorrow is a part of life. If we have the courage to feel the presence of sadness in our lives, to admit that we really love someone, or to acknowledge that something is very important to us, we can release the heaviness of sadness. In doing so, we create more space for being in the moment and allow room for new experiences.

The next chapter details shame: what it is and what it is not.

EIGHT

 *Shame*

Emotional Paralysis

A lot has been written about shame, which paralyzes, and guilt, which motivates. Both are addressed here because shame is one of the primary feelings, and it often gets confused with guilt.

Guilt is about having a conscience. When we know the difference between right and wrong, guilt is the natural outcome of feeling bad about doing wrong. It can be easy to rectify most mistakes we make. We admit what we did, apologize for our actions, and make it up to the other person, if possible. We ask for forgiveness and we forgive. Most of all, we change our behavior.

Guilt asks that we admit we have been hurtful to another. When we do, we free ourselves from the past and the guilt. We feel vulnerable when we admit our mistakes. We run the risk of being seen as imperfect and unlovable or of being misunderstood. However, many times, after telling someone "Yes, you're right. I was selfish. I'm sorry I broke my promise" or something similar, we inherit the unmistakable sense of emotional freedom. It is truly heady and beautiful. The energy of guilt and anxiety dissolve, and all is clear, clean, and fresh. The process is straightforward and tidy.

Shame, however, is neither tidy nor easy to disperse, as we will see.

The Guilt Continuum

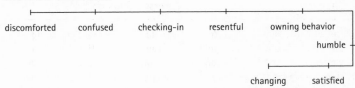

discomforted   confused   checking-in   resentful   owning behavior

humble

changing   satisfied

The Shame Continuums

Doing the Shaming

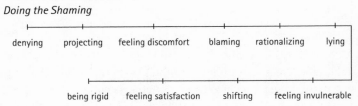

denying   projecting   feeling discomfort   blaming   rationalizing   lying

being rigid   feeling satisfaction   shifting   feeling invulnerable

Being Shamed

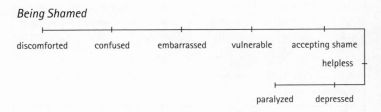

discomforted   confused   embarrassed   vulnerable   accepting shame

helpless

paralyzed   depressed

ABOUT SHAME

Shame is *not* the result of our doing something bad and feeling awful about it. Shame is the result of feeling responsible for something we *did not do,* which is why it is so paralyzing. How can we apologize for or change those things we haven't done? And why should we feel bad about what we haven't done? For example:

Shaming	Person Shamed
The shaming person says, "You are a baby. You are too old to be wetting the bed. What do you think your friends would say if they knew? Next time, you're really going to get it. I'll rub your face in those sheets."	Child feels there is something wrong with her that she can't change. She feels helpless and angry with herself because she can't stop. She is afraid others will find out and that she will have her face rubbed in the sheets. She has no one to turn to and may begin to believe she is not very good or lovable.
What's the Payoff for the Person Doing the Shaming?	**What the Child Learns from Being Shamed**
The shaming person feels powerful and in control. She may be doing what she learned. Now it is her turn to be in charge, to displace shame about a daughter's bed-wetting or her own issues onto another. Her ego is happy, but her heart is not.	Child develops a lack of trust in herself because she can't do what the adult asks. She sees herself as less than capable, and she is, in fact, less powerful. She suffers.
What Could Be Done Differently?	**What the Child Learns from Not Being Shamed**
A nonshaming person says, "It looks like you wet your bed last night. Is that right? How are you doing? Maybe we can figure out some ways to help you at night. Okay? I love you, honey. It's all right, sweetheart. It's not your fault. We can work on this together."	The child senses the other person is in her corner. She doesn't have to problem-solve on her own. She is hopeful that together they'll find a solution. Even though she doesn't like wetting the bed, she knows she can get help. She trusts another with her whole self.

THE ENERGY OF SHAME

A tremendous amount of energy is used in experiencing shame. At times we can feel the force of all that backed-up energy ready to surge up and out, like water pushing against a dam. This energy belongs to us. It holds enormous potential.

The energy of shame gets displaced when we blame others for our problems or when we are blamed for others' problems. For example, a manager sloughs off his responsibility for a mismanaged deal to a nonmanagement employee by saying, "She didn't complete the paperwork correctly." Or an abuser blames the victim for his actions, saying, "That kid wanted me to teach him about sex." Or an alcoholic declares, "I drink because my spouse is such a nag. And who wouldn't drink with kids like mine?"

When we refuse to take responsibility for our feelings and actions by pointing the finger at others, we shift our uncomfortable energy onto them. If they are naive, unaware, or unable to stand up for themselves, then the exchange seems like a success. We walk away, leaving others with our blame. They now carry not only shame but also outrage and a sense of unfairness. They may question themselves, and if they are not emotionally whole, they may experience a floating sense of nameless doubt that ends in questions about being lovable. No wonder we can easily paralyze those we shame.

When we shame another, we do not release the pent-up energy. We only shift our current self-loathing or discomfort onto another temporarily. It seems like we succeed because the energy is directed at another. However, we will need to unburden ourselves again before long. Shaming is being *emotionally irresponsible,* and it does not bring contentment, satisfaction, or peace. Taking responsibility for our emotions and actions is the only way to free ourselves, so that the energy used to resist responsibilities becomes available for the business of living.

ADULTS SHAMING ADULTS

Shaming happens in adulthood. Many of us whose childhoods were shame-based find it hard to deal with being wounded in the same old places. Sometimes we become more helpless. Shaming is a form of bullying and abuse. We need to recognize, name, and return the emotional energy to those who shame us. Some of us need help asserting our boundaries. But learning how to do this is a lifelong process that frees us from being emotionally paralyzed and prevents us from shaming others.

Many of us have been taught that judging others is wrong. But if we don't make certain judgments, we put ourselves at risk.

Unhealthy judgments come from the ego. They are very natural to us, authoritative, and need our monitoring. These are judgments about who or what is superior or inferior. These judgments include ideas or statements such as "She is not pretty," "He is not as good a ballplayer as he thinks," or " I am much better than he is."

Necessary judgments come from thoroughly comparing, discerning, and penetrating to the truth. This type of judgment is important for understanding the nature of someone who is shaming us. When the words don't match the reality, then we make a judgment that something is untrue. When the source is not honest, then we base our interactions on that understanding. We carefully judge the circumstances, but we are not judgmental.

THE ORIGINS OF SHAME

Shame is typically imposed on us by people close to us. Children are often shamed for things that, while frustrating for some parents, are just part of the growing and learning process. Children make many mistakes, from wetting their pants to spilling milk.

Out of these mistakes, children learn and evolve. Sometimes parents take children's innocent and necessary mistakes as personal affronts to their authority or as poor reflections of their parenting skills. They shame children for forgetting a chore, whining, or being self-concerned. When we shame these types of behaviors, we aren't considering our child's development, safety, and unfolding. We simply impose control.

Another trying time that can end in shame occurs when children say "no." The need to say "no" is a big developmental step for children. It is the beginning of learning how to take responsibility for what they need and want. If children do not learn to say "no" or if they say "no" but are ignored or shamed, they learn that opinions, thoughts, and feelings are unimportant.

Shaming a child differs from disciplining a child. In exercising discipline—a form of loving teaching—we set limits, share information, and have objective reasons for teaching the lesson. We teach the child how to substitute safer, more helpful behaviors.

When parents or teachers shame children, the behavior they want changed may not be specified. When an adult reacts or overreacts to a child's behavior, what the child learns may be confusing. For example, if a teacher shames a child by choosing to punish him or her for something everyone in the class is doing, the children in the classroom see the teacher as being moody. The focus shifts from their behavior to the teacher's behavior, and the point is lost. When we do not specify our reasons for wanting a particular activity done or refrained from, we put others in the unfortunate position of needing to read our mind. Expectations of mind reading, while sometimes unintentional, can also be intentional and used as a battering ram.

The origins of shame, when we discover them, usually show us how the shaming message is really about the person pointing the finger at us. How to return that energy to the original owner is found in "Shame Exercises" on pages 132–134.

FEAR-BASED SHAMING

In families that hold religious beliefs, adults need to help their children know the difference between making a mistake and committing a *sin* (an offense against God). If we tell a child his behavior is sinful, what is our intent? Are we trying to intimidate the child so he will be afraid to make mistakes, or are we trying to teach him to have internal control over his life by giving him consequences for his actions? Teaching children to integrate morality into their lives does not need to include spiritual shame, which is based on fear.

For example, when a child takes a cookie after being told not to, we may say, "God is watching you. You should be ashamed of yourself. Now you have hurt God by stealing a cookie, and God doesn't love you anymore." The message to the child is that he is powerful, so powerful he can hurt God, and so bad that he can make God stop loving him. The child becomes confused as to what he's done wrong. Is it the lying, the stealing, the hurting God, having God's love withdrawn, or something else? What should he change?

With spiritual shame, a child may deduce that the only reason not to lie or steal is because "God is watching." And while this may work as long as he believes in a watching God, what happens if his beliefs change? This locus of control for his behavior is not from within him. We want children to grow into adults who have morals and a conscience from the inside out. We want them to base their behavior on what they know and believe to be right, not on what they feel ashamed about.

If the child is told, "When you take cookies without asking, I feel that I can't trust you. I want to trust you. Because you took

the cookie without asking, you cannot have one for dessert."
The child's thinking will be focused on his behavior instead of
on God, punishment, or the parent's emotions. The locus of control stays in the child's corner.

In terms of childhood development, threats about sin may
not be as effective as information shared in a loving and caring
manner. If we want our child to learn about divine love, we can
educate him about spiritual ideas in safety, not in the middle of
a volatile moment that may have more to do with our anger
than with our child's error. Staying aware of our own feelings
and our behavior when we correct our child is as important as
keeping an eye on his behavior.

Linda's Story

Linda's father was a grocer who had hoped to move on
to a white-collar job. Linda's mother was a hair stylist.
Between their incomes, they managed to get by. When
Linda began doing well in grade school, she became the
family hero. They began to feel she could do no wrong.
Linda became the symbol and bearer of the family's hope
for a bigger, better life. Her performance in school was
promising, her teachers said. Linda's parents told her she
was making them proud in the community, as well as at
home. When Linda got less than a B+, her parents were
less congratulatory. Linda began thinking she was responsible for her parents' happiness. When they said, "The
whole world knows how proud we are of you," Linda
heard, through the limitations of her adolescent experience, that her performance in school was the source of her
parents' happiness.

As Linda began taking more difficult high school
classes, she discovered she did not always know how to
solve her homework problems. She felt paralyzed and

couldn't ask for help. In her belief system, not being perfect would imply shame for her family. She was also ashamed at how little she understood. When she failed to get perfect grades, Linda felt helpless to correct her situation and she began to numb out.

As her sophomore year progressed, Linda fell behind. She found excuses not to show her parents her grades. She lied to them about her success and worried constantly about what would happen when they found out she was letting them down. She was afraid her failure would make her unlovable and humiliate her parents. Linda became silent and depressed.

Linda saw her image and her life spiraling out of control. In the privacy of her bedroom, Linda began making small cuts on her arms. She couldn't verbally ask for help, but she could control her emotional pain through physical means. She created an outlet.

Linda's shame was paralyzing. It drove her to silence. Her silence nearly drove her to suicide. Her school counselor suggested she get counseling. The therapist wisely involved Linda's parents in working through separation and boundary issues, as well as in learning ways to communicate. Linda attended a group that mirrored realistic and specific responses to her behavior. Eventually, Linda overcame her paralysis.

Adolescence is a difficult time to learn to ask for help if being vulnerable has led to shame. The underlying relationship between child and parent becomes more visible during this time. If shame is part of the emotional foundation for the adolescent, whose developmental job is now to pull away from parents and make mistakes, he or she

will be on shaky ground. Appropriate mirroring and specific information give adolescents solid support.

TAKING EMOTIONAL RESPONSIBILITY

When parents take responsibility for their own hopes, dreams, and failures, they see their son or daughter as a child, not someone playing the hero. When parents take responsibility for their own disappointments, they free their children from the burden of fulfilling a prescribed role. When each parent is emotionally responsible, other family members are allowed to grow and change.

Honest interactions create a haven. Wisdom comes from making honest mistakes, from having the mistakes mirrored back with new information added, and from learning more effective ways of being in the world. Shame distorts and truncates this otherwise natural process.

Shame is a circle. When we have been shamed, we tend to shame others. If we don't recognize our shame-based behaviors, we tend to make up rules for others. These rules become very important to us, and those who do not live by our rules are subject to punishment, if we have the power to inflict it. These rules can deal with any issue: Real men don't cry. Real women are always loving. You must have a perfect body. Real men have sex with women they don't care about. If you love him, you must give in to him. If you make mistakes, you must be a loser. If your parents don't have money, you're a loser. If you don't go to college, you're a loser.

So many of these rules come out of personalities or situations over which we have no control. These sorts of rules are simply wrong. Men of all kinds do cry. Women aren't always loving. No one has a perfect body, and everyone has a perfect body. We do not have control over the cloudy subjective opinions of others. Being lovable is in the eye of the beholder. Being poor is in the eye of the beholder. Being perfect is in the eye of the beholder.

Each of these rules is a judgment. Each judgment is an opinion often coming from a hidden bias. Not knowing what the bias is but hearing the judgment can leave us needing to defend ourselves. But from what? Not knowing the answer to that question can lead back to feeling ashamed. If the bias were known, we could easily say to ourselves, "That person has failed at many things. He really thinks *he* is the loser. His judgment is really about him." Whether we say it aloud or to ourselves, we give back the energy of shame by acknowledging that the judgment is about the person doing the shaming.

When we shame others, we make judgments in order to avoid the original wound of shame. We shame others in order not to be shamed. We shame others in order not to let them know we have been shamed. We shame others to get the focus off us and onto them.

When we are shamed, we can end up hating ourselves even though it is irrational. We still feel somehow that we must be at fault. Shame can also cause us to believe that we are unworthy and unable to achieve important goals or put our natural gifts to use. It's not surprising that we need help getting a perspective on shame. When we get to the base of shame, we find we are suffering sorrow, anger, and fear—all of which can be released.

With help, we can learn that we are helpless to change how someone thinks about us. We become clearly able to differentiate between what belongs to another person and what is ours to change. Once the energy dissipates, we are no longer pushed to say harmful shaming words to others or especially to ourselves. Peace and acceptance replace shame. Tolerance and understanding replace shame. Boundaries and interdependence replace shame. Self-appreciation and self-love replace shame. Action and satisfaction replace shame.

SHAME EXERCISES

You can move away from the paralysis of shame. You can identify shame through the emotional inventory on pages 163–167. Doing an inventory will help you resurrect old shame and release some of its energy, as well as learn how to refuse shame-based messages from others.

The exercises that follow here will help you become aware of shame that is more current. If you want to continue working with your emotional vocabulary, read over all the exercises here and start on them today. Continue to write in the notebook designated for learning about your emotions. Put your exercises in one place so you can see both your patterns and your solutions over time.

1. Spend two days noting whenever you feel shame or inappropriate responsibility for someone else's behavior.
2. Make three columns in your notebook, labeling them as shown in the example that follows. Fill in the columns with events from your own experience.

Caution: When working through issues of shame, you may mistakenly interpret another's words or behaviors as shaming. For example, if you feel ashamed of your body, you need to understand that not all comments about your body are meant to be shaming. For a more accurate perspective, talk to a friend about your thoughts and reactions.

What Was Said	What Was the Message	How I Feel
I was called an idiot by my teacher.	The message to me was that I am stupid and incapable, that I am a loser and will not be able to succeed.	I still feel embarrassed because all the kids laughed at me. I still feel sad because it hurt my feelings. I still feel angry because I couldn't help not understanding the math problem.
My father called me stupid.	The message to me was that there is something wrong with me, that there is something wrong with my thinking.	I still feel sad. I was so hurt that my own father would say that. I was angry and hated myself. I was scared because there was no one to protect me. I was scared because my father didn't seem to love me and because I didn't know how to "fix" myself.

Once you see what the message is, figure out whom the message is really about and reframe the shaming information to a more realistic and helpful message, as seen in the example that follows.

Who the Message Is About	Returning the Message	Reframing the Message
My teacher did not control her temper. She was verbally abusive to me.	That message is about my teacher. It is not about me. I am fine. I can let go of this message. I forgive her.	I am intelligent. I am capable. I am a winner and successful in many ways.
My father was unhappy. He was cruel to me.	That message is about my father. He wanted to go to college, but he didn't. It is not about me. I can let go of his message and will work on releasing my desire to punish him.	I can list the ways in which I am intelligent. I am healthy. I am lovable. I can protect myself from cruelty. I follow my intellectual inclinations and enjoy them.

Go through the list about whom the message was really about and note how you feel about the person, the message, and yourself. List your feelings and discover where you failed to protect yourself. Release the anger and fear. Make a plan to do things differently next time.

3. When you go through a shame attack that paralyzes, call a friend and talk through the experience until you get some distance. Return to these shame exercises and work through them as needed.

MOVING FORWARD

When we get to the bottom of shame, to the underlying messages, we often find the information is ridiculous or very clearly has to do with the other person. When we discover what is actually being said, we name it, return the responsibility for it, and reframe and affirm the truth about ourselves. Healing these often silent and paralyzing shadowy whispers may release the fear and anger that have kept us in unhealthy relationships and from pursuing dreams and hopes for love.

On the other hand, rolling our eyes, pointing our finger, making blanket statements, or taking feelings out on others are clues that we're not handling shame in a healthy way. If we acknowledge shame, we take risks, face fears, and find out the truth. Working through shame slowly and with support will bring a balanced perspective about who we are, and it will give us self-confidence.

The next chapter describes how to get back to earlier curiosity, interests, and joy through honest communication.

NINE

🦋 *Communication Skills*
Putting the Concepts into Practice

Communication skills are the tools that let us release emotions practically and effectively. We have learned *what* emotional energy is and *why* we need to release it. Communication skills are the *where* and the *how*.

Communicating can either escalate conflict or bring understanding and solutions. Communicating involves sharing perceptions and feelings with someone else. When we do this effectively, we draw closer through building trust, fostering respect, and creating an environment of learning—about others and ourselves.

Communication skills help us with the more intimate and friendly relationships in which we already have trust, as well as with day-to-day situations with our colleagues, co-workers, acquaintances, and strangers. This chapter details communication skills and suggestions that set the stage for releasing emotional energy, old and new.

SITUATIONAL EMOTIONS

We react to our worlds. Sometimes this involves situations instead of people. *Situational* emotion has its source in events and institutions, and it is caused by unknown or inaccessible forces.

When we experience emotions related to events rather than people, we still need to release the energy. If we go through a personal disaster, such as a storage area getting flooded, we may experience strong feelings. Whom do we blame? The water? God? The floodplain? Ourselves? Where do we focus the feelings? We need to acknowledge these feelings as they arise. To do this, we can connect our feelings to the situation and ask someone to listen to us. For example:

Jill: This is not about you, Greg, but I am so sad that we lost that storage shed. I am just heartbroken about those family photos. They are gone forever! I loved that one picture of Grandpa and me so much. I can't believe it happened. I feel helpless! I wish I could talk to Grandpa now. He'd know what to do.

Greg: I know those pictures meant the world to you. Of course you're really sad. I'm sorry, too, that you lost your treasures, especially that picture of you and your grandfather.

GETTING TRIGGERED

Sometimes the emotions we feel, while caused by what is going on now, are really more closely tied to the past. In communicating how we feel in these situations, we need to be able to do two things: (1) acknowledge that we are being affected here and now and (2) acknowledge that our reaction may have more to do with what happened in the past.

Raeleen's Story

Raeleen was usually picked on about her looks just as she was leaving for school. Her mother couldn't seem to help finding that one flaw to nag Raeleen about. Now, Raeleen is happily married. Many mornings, just as she's rushing off to work, she feels anxious when her husband tries to kiss her good-bye. Raeleen feels shame when her husband looks into her face as she's leaving. He is surprised at Raeleen's turning away from him, but for her, this situation sets off old emotional land mines.

Raeleen can figure out the ingredients of her situation:

1. She sees that old energy is getting triggered and that her husband is not to blame.
2. She needs to be honest with her husband about what's going on.
3. She needs to deal with her feelings about both present and past events.

Raeleen Gets Honest about Her Feelings

Here is a way for Raeleen to begin:

Raeleen: Sweetheart, this is about me and not about you.

Robert: What is it?

Raeleen: Well, I feel so ashamed when you try to kiss me right as I'm going out. The shame is not about you. I think it's so familiar and uncomfortable because I had to put up with my mother scanning how I looked and being criticized as I was going out the door. I can't seem to help it.

Robert: So, you feel ashamed when I try to kiss you good-bye?

Raeleen: Yes.

Robert: Wow! That's too bad, because you always look so beautiful to me. What do you expect me to do?

Raeleen: Well, I'd appreciate if we could just try kissing ten minutes before I leave.

Robert: Sure. We can do that.

Raeleen: Thanks so much. It is a good reminder for me to take care of this. I couldn't confront my mother about it back then, but I can do something about it now. I want to be able to kiss you as I leave.

Robert: Well, I am just so sorry you see yourself through her eyes. I'll do what I can to support you. I love kissing you!

Raeleen: Yes, I know, honey. That's one of the big reasons for wanting to take care of it. I don't want her stuff clogging up our relationship! Thank you.

Raeleen's situational shame belongs to her and her mother, not to the innocent bystander who triggers it. When we communicate with others about getting triggered, we can say, "This is not about you." That takes the other person off the hook and frees him or her to listen and support us.

Raeleen Takes Responsibility for Changing Her Environment

The second part to resolving this issue also belongs to Raeleen. She is responsible for taking action to resolve the situation. For example, Raeleen needs to

1. prepare and return the shameful statements to her mother at some point through an emotional inventory, whether she shares the specifics with her mother or not

2. replace her mother's ideas with her own supportive, specific, and realistic thoughts: I am a responsible, dependable person who is going off to work. I am loved by my terrific husband. I feel great! I look fine now and always have.

There is a difference between owning our feelings in these situations and blaming another for "making us feel this way." We need to take responsibility for our feelings and release those that are current as well as those from the past that continue getting triggered. And we need to take actions to support changes we are making.

MAKING SOMEONE FEEL A CERTAIN WAY: TRUTH OR FANTASY?

It has been said that no one can make us feel a certain way, whether angry, ashamed, sad, glad, or scared. This is not always true. When we trust others, when we love others, when we have an understanding with others, and when we make commitments and promises to others, we are vulnerable.

Some people do have the power to hurt us. We give them that power because we let them into our lives and into our heart. When someone we love or care about is cruel to us, we feel hurt. When someone we love is hurt by circumstances or others, we often hurt as well. When someone we love dies, we are devastated.

While others may sometimes have power to hurt us, they

cannot make us *act out* our sorrow, anger, shame, or fear. All the energy from our feelings belongs to us. These emotions are our legacy, and they contribute something solid and unique to our lives. When we can let go of the resistance, we will build something for ourselves instead. That energy is ours.

So, others can make us feel something, but after that, *we* choose. We think about what we want to do that will ennoble and enrich our lives. We act on the energy in our time, in our way, and to our benefit. This is what personal power is all about.

A SPECIAL KIND OF CYCLE

Many of us have at least one person in our lives who chronically hurts us. Whether this is a family member, friend, spouse, child, colleague, or neighbor, we care about this person and are vulnerable to his or her actions and words. But with practice, we can become less vulnerable. We can step back after having been hurt or after having unsuccessfully attempted to work out a mutually acceptable way of dealing with one another. We can then make a plan to reduce our vulnerability, to remove our heart from the front line. We say to ourselves, "She is doing this because of . . ." We begin to take the words and actions less personally, even if they are intended to be personal. Each time we do this, we step out of the way emotionally. For example, if our words get twisted and turned against us, we withdraw from sharing information that can be twisted. We may limit the amount of time we spend with the other person. We may outgrow our vulnerability by seeing words and actions for what they are: statements that often come from unhealed wounds, which have nothing to do with us. Many times, people who continually try to hurt us have undiagnosed instabilities that need treatment.

Over time, we create better techniques for sidestepping the

emotional bait that may have kept us in pain. We talk with others to get support and ideas.

TALKING AND THE PAST

Sometimes our desire to communicate goes awry. We add fuel to the fire unintentionally. Wanting to communicate effectively is the first step, but being able to do so takes some restraint and practice. We may not be able to communicate everything we want—not at the beginning and maybe not ever. We need to practice staying in the moment and focusing on present events.

Miscommunication can occur when we create long lists of past misunderstandings, when we hang out our "dirty laundry." This decreases the chance of resolving present issues because the past often includes trying to be right, plotting revenge, polarizing right and wrong, and attempting to win. These are powerful agendas that take the focus away from the present.

Miscommunication can also occur when we use the word *always*. This word carries a lot of energy and power. Our relationships with others may have patterns of miscommunication. The word *always* may resurrect our old pool of emotions, and we may begin to re-experience that whole emotional history. This energy can feel huge, overwhelming, dangerous, disgusting, and too complicated to deal with.

Miscommunication also occurs when we say words that are hard to take back. Sometimes the person we feel hurt by ought not be the first person we talk to, especially in cases of *old* or *big* emotions. We need to be cautious about how much of the past we delve into, and we ought to know what our goals are. There is nothing wrong with agreeing on guidelines for discussing past issues. But both parties need to be clear about these guidelines.

When the past must be sorted and cleared in order to discover whether love and respect are still possible, we seek professional help with a good facilitator. A facilitator will help us learn communication skills that not only release old emotional charges in safety but also help us maintain healthy relationships.

DECIDING WHOM TO SHARE WITH

We need to be cautious before we sit down to a discussion. Each of us comes to the table with different beliefs or desires. We need to listen, negotiate, and ask questions. Sometimes the goals are not workable. If others have a track record of wanting to blame, be victimized, stay stuck in a no-win communication style (like venting), are unwilling, or want us to reinforce how tough their lives are, then we decide whether we want to invest in talking with them.

If we decide to have a conversation, we can start by clarifying our reasons for wanting to get together. For example:

Mark: I would really like to get together to talk about the argument we had last week.

Sylvia: Why? So we can have the same argument all over again?

Mark: No. I'm trying to understand the reasons we have these same disagreements over and over. I thought maybe we could just have a cup of coffee together and share our perceptions and opinions about it. I'd like to try.

Sylvia: Well, I don't think it's going to work.

Mark: I'm not sure either, but I want to try.

Sylvia: Okay, I'm willing to give it a shot.

Now, if Mark had not really wanted Sylvia's participation, he would have focused on her attitude by saying, "If you're going to be nasty, forget it." Instead, Mark's goal was to do things differently, and he did not let the old pattern of defending himself get in the way. He chose to look past the closed door and seek an opening.

For someone who has been terribly victimized and is continuing to live in a destructive situation, developing the courage to make changes can require countless exchanges, reviews, and reframing. If we don't have the tools, understanding, or patience to be there for a person with this history, then we can suggest in a loving way that we are not equipped to deal with the issues. We can then suggest that he or she seek professional help.

CHOOSING OUR WORDS

There is usually no need for us to go for the jugular when we are agreeing to listen, understand, and take responsibility for our role in a misunderstanding. If we're dealing with a friend, spouse, child, relative, or someone else we care about, we want understanding and a win-win resolution. We may, out of habit or desire, use certain inflammatory words in an argument to bulk up our side. These words, while giving us a greater sense of power, are guaranteed to escalate the misunderstanding.

Pushing-away words: you, never, always, should, absolutely, did, must (as in "You know that you absolutely wanted to hurt me!")

Bringing-closer words: I, seems like, seemed to, often, may, might, maybe, perhaps (as in "Perhaps you didn't know how late I was going to be. Maybe I did forget to tell you.")

Providing leeway for others to work with us toward a solution, rather than trying to wrest their answers from them, offers mutual trust and higher expectations.

Each person involved in two-way communication is not necessarily 50 percent responsible for problems, only 50 percent responsible for resolving them.

USING THE WORD *I*

To create give-and-take in relationships, we must be willing to have a relationship with ourselves. How do we do that? One of the easiest ways is using the little word *I*. When we want to discuss feelings, we say, "I feel mad (sad, glad, scared, or ashamed) when that happens."

If we begin that same sentence with *you, he,* or *she,* we create distance from the immediacy of the energy. The energetic emotion is now in us, regardless of the source of the emotion. For example, if a neighbor accidentally runs over a bicycle belonging to our child, we feel angry. We may be angry with the child for leaving it in the neighbor's driveway; we may be angry that the neighbor was not more careful when backing out; and we may be angry with ourselves for not checking on the bike's location. The table on page 147 shows what happens if we stay at the "blame the neighbor" level.

What goes on internally is a *sorting* process. We initially think that the other person is to blame. We think, "You make me mad." We say to ourselves, "Of course it's your fault, you jerk. Look where you're going next time and pay me for my kid's bike!" We are human. We can have these reactions, but what's important is how we *choose* to express them. We can choose words that let us take responsibility for how we feel. When the

What We Say	What They Say	What Happens
"You make me mad. Why did you do that?"	"It's not my fault. It's your kid's fault." (Most people defend themselves when attacked.)	We feel more frustrated because we can't get through to the neighbor. This makes it even harder to let go or get compensation for the bike.

time comes for talking about it, we can do so with restraint and nonspecific expectations. We can stay open to negotiation.

When we use *I* to tell our stories, we are talking about ourselves. These are our feelings. We choose to get down and dirty with them, own them, feel them, acknowledge them, and release them. If we keep our distance, as though these feelings are the fault of and, therefore, belong to the person whose actions are at the source, we remain helpless to do anything about the energy.

One of the most natural things in the world is to want the person who hurt us to feel our pain. We can admit that to ourselves and others, but then we must get on with the business of taking care of our emotional lives. It takes time and energy and faith to believe that the pain won't last forever. In the end, going through the process of releasing our emotions changes us, and we can and usually do move on. We start by owning responsibility for our feelings by saying "I."

THE GROUND RULES

When we decide to talk to someone about a problem, we need a level playing field. Both parties can agree to ground rules. For example:

General Considerations	Example
We will agree on our goal.	We would like to resolve the misunderstanding about last Friday night.
We will listen to one another and reflect back.	We each get to state our version of what we thought happened.
We will take responsibility for how we feel.	We will say "I" and not blame the other person.
We will keep our focus on this incident.	We won't bring up what happened last Wednesday night.
We will agree on a plan to resolve the issue.	We won't walk out no matter how angry we get, and we won't resort to swearing. We will work at it until we get to an understanding and solution.

During the discussion, each person listens to the other person without distractions. This sort of discussion is meant to be a safe place for us to learn how to talk about our emotional realities. We learn how our opinions differ from our emotions. We learn that another person can have feelings that we are not responsible for. These discussions help us learn. We learn more about those we love and vice versa. We also learn something about ourselves because we don't need to gear up for a fight in which we have to defend ourselves.

INTENTIONS

When we are ready to communicate about something important, we ask ourselves questions in order to clarify our intentions:

- Do we need to "win" the argument in order to make discussion worth our while?
- Do we want to understand what's going on?
- Do we want to "fix" the situation so all will be peaceful?
- Do we want to vent at the other person?
- Do we want to punish, get revenge, or push the other person away?
- Do we want to open up the relationship and try new ways of relating?

Communication that furthers relationships is kept in the here and now, unless special time has been set aside to discuss past issues.

ASKING FOR A MEETING

When we become aware that we are overreacting to something, or that our emotions are not reasonable compared to the actual situation, then we ask for a *meeting*. We ask for meetings whether the feelings are big or small, new or old. Meetings give us a place to focus on acknowledging our emotions. Meetings are not for blaming or defending a position. Initially, it is a good idea to schedule meetings often until we get into the habit of identifying and sharing feelings together. Meetings give us a chance to practice working through both small and big issues, bringing more awareness to the good in our lives and in us. We start with just a two-person meeting and may gradually expand the group.

Although all these steps may seem formal and like too much trouble, by practicing them a few times, we soon get to the point where our words for feelings and our listening skills become easier to engage. We begin casually asking for meetings anytime we begin to feel a groundswell of emotion. We can have meetings over the phone, in public, or at home (although having meetings while traveling in a car is not a good idea). There are many places for meetings in which we can focus completely on communicating.

THE IMPORTANCE OF PLACE IN A MEETING

Location is important to meetings. We need to find a place that both people agree is not a trigger for defensiveness. Initially, by choosing a location for emotional exchanges, we *contain* our discussion of issues. By discussing issues only in our chosen location, we contain how much our emotions crowd our day. Instead of going over how we will defend ourselves when the other person says something, we can relax. We can keep an open mind. We will have the opportunity to express how *we* feel. There is freedom in knowing we don't have to be ready to discuss issues at any point in the day. We can wait until we are ready.

We need to find a neutral place to talk. If we tend to fight in the living room, we don't have our meeting there, or in *her* studio, *his* office, or the kids' rooms. Kitchens are often fairly nonproprietary places. We can make an appointment, make tea, and make ourselves the priority. It is important to refrain from using alcohol, drugs, or other substances that may contribute to a distorted perspective.

LISTENING IN THE MEETING

Listening is an activity. Listening means actively clearing our mind of ideas other than those of the present moment. Listening means putting our own feelings, thoughts, responses, reactions, wants, needs, and fears on hold while we consider the other person. Easy to say, but not always easy to do. In the meeting, we listen to the other person's emotional realities. We may want to begin by keeping the initial meetings short, perhaps two minutes long if we think of ourselves as beginners. We can lengthen the time of the meeting as our listening abilities increase.

We meet as equals: two people with feelings who pull together in support of one another. Should we find ourselves wanting revenge, making judgments, wanting to argue with the other person's feelings, we simply notice our ideas and opinions and return to listening. It doesn't matter whether we think the other person is right or wrong. It doesn't matter whether we want to win, or whether we think or know that we are right, or whether we feel hateful. All we need to do is listen. Once the other person finishes talking, we repeat his or her emotional reality back to him or her with as much care and accuracy as we can muster.

PUTTING THE CONCEPTS INTO PRACTICE:
AN EXAMPLE

Lisa and Bob have been married for several years. They have three children and are very busy. Lately, they have been abrupt with one another and unable to forgive. In this meeting at their home, they try to listen.

Lisa: I am angry that I didn't get a raise. I've been at that counter selling too long to be passed over again. I am really angry with my boss! I am angry when I get home and see how many chores I have to do before I go to bed. All I want to do is relax! I was really scared on my way home tonight because some kid ran out into the street right in front of me. I was sure I couldn't stop soon enough. It scared the hell out of me! I'm not only angry but also hurt that my boss didn't get me the raise.

Bob: So, let's see . . . you are angry that you didn't get the raise you deserve. You're scared that some kid ran out in front of the car. And you're angry that there's so much that has to be done in the house before we go to bed. Did I miss anything?

Lisa: Yes, I feel hurt that my boss didn't stand up for me, that he didn't make an effort to get me a raise!

Bob: You're hurt that your boss didn't go to bat to get you that raise. Is that it?

Lisa: Yeah. Now it's your turn.

Then Bob goes on to his feelings. Notice he didn't argue with Lisa about how she felt. He didn't tell her *not* to feel that way. He didn't interrupt and say, "Your boss is a jerk!" He didn't add, "You were probably driving too fast in that kid's neighborhood. Didn't I tell you before that someday you'd get into trouble?" Bob did none of these. Instead, he listened and reflected back what he heard, like a friendly mirror.

Some days the list of issues will be long. Some days the feelings will be about others. Some days the feelings will be about the person listening to us. When this happens, we may find it harder to share and harder to listen. Some days plans will need to be made around the feelings. The foundation for planning gets established as we learn how to let go. And as we really hear and begin to understand those we love, we will develop more trust, respect, and love.

By listening, we help others release some of the energy related to their day, which frees them up to be more available to themselves, others, and us. We participate in one another's lives, which brings trust, closeness, and practice in how to be mature, responsible, and more fully engaged in life.

Some meetings may look like the following:

Bob: Could we please have a meeting after dinner?

Lisa: I can do it right now, if you can.

Bob: Great. The sooner the better.

Bob can ask for a meeting before he gets too angry about something, especially when he knows it's not really about anything Lisa is doing. When Bob realizes that he is reacting to the past, as well as to Lisa right now, he can say something like the following:

Bob: Lisa, I know I am feeling furious, and it's not about you. I am angry with you because you forgot to mail my payment in and now it may be late, but I'm feeling a lot more anger than just about the bill. Maybe if we have a meeting, I'll be able to figure it out.

Lisa: You feel angry with me because I forgot to mail your payment. I'm sorry. I was just in such a rush that I forgot. I'll call them to see whether we can pay directly from the account. We can have a meeting in about fifteen minutes. Can you wait?

Bob: I don't want to hear about your reasons right now. I just want to know that you've heard me.

Lisa: Yes, you feel angry with me and you'd like a meeting.

Bob: Yes. Thank you.

These communication tools (asking for a meeting and recognizing, naming, sharing, and releasing emotions) have stood the test of time. They are tried-and-true methods that work if both persons agree on the goals.

If the person we'd like to talk with doesn't want to meet with us, we can still take care of ourselves, either by writing in a journal or talking with a trusted friend. The most important aspect is that we access our emotions and release them.

UNWILLING MEETING PARTNERS

When the person we most want to speak with and share our feelings with is *not* interested or willing to try, we are put in a position of needing to create other emotional outlets. Being unable to share emotions with someone important to us can be very painful, but there are many ways to effectively take care of ourselves.

1. If we suspect that someone's pattern indicates more than just a bad day or the occasional dark mood, we begin to notice clues and patterns that might point to mental health issues. We may need to ask for professional opinions or assistance.
2. We accept the other person's resistance and turn our energy away from him or her.
3. We go to an appropriate support group or chat room, or we enlist friends and community resources to help us with suggestions, which we try.

4. We get honest with ourselves about how limited we will let our lives become before we disengage from the other person.

5. We set consequences and stick to them.

6. We look at the effect this other person is having on our family and us and determine how far we will let things go.

7. We don't accept abuse or neglect, whether for ourselves or for those we love.

8. We ask for divine guidance.

9. We write, talk, take walks, exercise, eat well, and care about ourselves.

10. We make a decision to let go of this person.

LETTING GO AND MOVING ON

As sad as it can be to let go of our expectations, it is even sadder when we lose track of ourselves in long-standing attempts at "fixing" another person. When we let go, we stay in touch with the relevance that our emotions play in the unfolding of our lives. Feeling emotions, understanding what they mean to us, and allowing them to change us bring us the potential for realizing emotional freedom, richness, trust, and maturity. Within our emotions are seeds of information. If we want to live life to its fullest, we use emotions as guides. Regardless of what those we love do or don't do, we stay in a relationship with our feelings.

Some people are afraid to write anything down because their partner does not respect their privacy. If this is the case, we can write in the car and see what falls onto the paper. Afterward, when we've worked through what was important, we can throw the paper away or burn it. We do what is safe.

If we are in a very unengaged place with someone we'd like to get closer to, we start by meeting in a public place with informal conversation. Eventually, we work up to telling someone things we enjoy about him or her. We find common ground and build on it without giving up our integrity. Over time, we may be able to work into a friendly focused meeting that will boost the relationship and resolve and heal the past.

COMMUNICATION EXERCISES

The exercises that follow will help you practice communicating effectively and building trusting relationships with yourself and others. For additional practice with recognizing emotions, see the emotional inventory on pages 163–167.

If you want to continue working with your emotional vocabulary, read over the exercises here and start on them today. Continue to write in the notebook designated for learning about your emotions and ask for meetings, as warranted.

1. You might want to role-play a meeting with a friend before you have an important actual meeting, in order to get practice and feedback. Then ask for a meeting.
2. Share three characteristics you like about yourself. The other person repeats what he or she heard.
3. Share five people or situations for which you feel grateful. The other person repeats your gratitude list.
4. Share one happy moment, funny idea, beautiful situation, or silly event that happened during the day. The other person repeats your story with a focus on your feelings.

These meetings are not the place to share old and grievous issues, especially when you are new to the process. Try to stay focused on recent developments. In time, you will know whether you are ready to deal with old and very difficult issues. You may want to share these with the other person in the presence of a clergyperson, therapist, or trained facilitator.

MOVING FORWARD

When I first used some of these exercises, I felt foolish, inept, and angry that I had to use a formula to have a conversation with someone. It was not easy to risk being vulnerable by asking for a meeting. Thank goodness, in time, I was able to improvise and make these techniques work for me. Now they have become second nature. I am able to keep my relationships fresh, clear, honest, and flexible. When I have something tough to say, I find it much easier to do so without a backlog. It works.

Life is much freer and easier when the emotional buck stops with us. We take the emotional hit, and we revitalize our lives.

TEN

Moving On
Wrapping Up

This book provides a new way of viewing our lives and the world around us. It gives us a tool kit with which to enjoy the energy that comes from emotions.

We can look beyond this book for other very helpful ideas and assistance:

1. Join an appropriate chat group. The Internet can be a treasure trove of help.
2. See a therapist. Therapists and trained facilitators have the tools to help us in safety through skipped developmental stages. Even if we did not have the opportunity earlier, we can face and overcome fears and obstacles now.
3. Make an appointment with a hypnotherapist, acupuncturist, acupressurist, or therapeutic allergist who can help you clear energy blocks. These treatments can be very effective. Make sure that the professional has been trained and is certified to treat clients.
4. Pray in your own way. There has been plenty of research done on the transforming and transmuting of energy as a result of prayer. Try it alone or with others. Prayer has been found to work across time and distance.

WELCOME TO THE WORLD OF PARADOX

Feelings can be very contradictory. Did you ever feel rage toward your parents? Did those feelings cancel out all the love you have for them—past, present, and future? If you're interested in experiencing feelings, you may also discover that you can hold two truths simultaneously. Shades of gray work well for human relationships. Contradictory and paradoxical experiences happen to most of us. For example:

- We go on living when someone we love is dying.
- The sun shines and seasons change in wartime.
- The person we divorce often still has the same qualities we initially fell in love with.
- People in positions of emotional, spiritual, or political authority are sometimes the worst abusers.
- We love our pets knowing that in all likelihood we will outlive them.
- We fall in love with no guarantees.
- We get so-called fatal illnesses, but we continue to wake, laugh, and love until the end.
- We say we love a God who wants us to act in loving ways, but then go ahead and do whatever we want.

We may not talk about these paradoxes, but we live them. Paradoxes are part of how we are built as humans. Believing in life's certainties is useful because it helps us to create guidelines, but expecting that our opinion about others will never change or that people are all good or all bad sets us up for disappointment. To believe that we will always feel either hatred or love is also unrealistic. That's why being in the moment and open to our feelings is essential. That's why acknowledging the not-so-good along with the good in others and ourselves allows for the flow of energy. Paradox does not call for us to be rigid, right, and emotionally entitled. Paradox invites freedom, change, and human evolution and development.

Now that you have some tips for taking responsibility for your emotions and you know emotions hold energy, you may find it easier to flow along and enjoy the variety.

I wish you emotional and energetic freedom, self-love, and generosity of spirit.

Taking an Emotional Inventory

In most recovery programs, people are encouraged to make emotional inventories. Emotional inventories list questions that help us take stock of our lives. It is helpful to inventory *all* the basic emotions. Doing this helps us sort out emotional ingredients and understand our wants, needs, and behavior patterns. Once we clearly see our behavior patterns, we can replace non-productive beliefs and actions with more effective responses.

This is not to say that we must go back and revisit every feeling we've ever had. When we begin working on patterns and releasing some of the emotional energy, it is like removing stones from a dam. We do not need to remove all of the stones in order to relieve pressure and let the water flow freely.

1. Before beginning an inventory about any emotion, set aside time and get focused. Turn off the television and unplug the phone, because getting at emotional information takes quiet time and space to reflect, remember, and feel. Determine the emotion you'd like to inventory, such as sorrow, and consider it for a while.

2. Take a pen and paper and write down what your inventory will focus on: "Sorrow Inventory," for example. Make two columns. In the first column, put

the word "Person" or "Institution" or "Event" as the heading. In the second column, use the words "My Story" as the heading.

3. Set that paper aside. On a second piece of paper, begin listing all the people, situations, and events you can think of related to the feeling you've chosen. It doesn't matter whether you are still close to a person or even whether a person is still alive. List all the people, situations, and events that evoke that feeling, whether today, yesterday, or thirty years ago. List them no matter what the nature of the emotion: small or large, old or new, justified or not. It may take several days to let the idea of the inventory sink in, so it is fine to take some time to add items to the list. When you are finished, look over the list and decide which person, situation, or event you are ready to work on. Fill in the columns you made in step 2. For example:

Sorrow Inventory

Event	My Story
Hurricane	I feel sad that my dog was taken away from me.
Institution	**My Story**
Government	I am sad that the laws have changed and that my uncle can't get enough help with his war injuries.
Person	**My Story**
Father	I am sad that he never knew who I am because he never had a real conversation with me.

4. After you have gone through the entire list of persons, institutions, and events in step 3, get a third sheet of paper and place it next to the "My Story" column. Make two columns on this new sheet of paper. Label the first column "How I Was Affected" and the other column "How I Can Change This Pattern."

   In the first column, list how you were affected by this person, situation, or event. Keep the possibilities limited to nine categories: physical, emotional, spiritual, mental, social, educational, cultural, financial, and sexual. For example:

   • How did this person affect me physically, emotionally, spiritually, mentally, socially, educationally, culturally, financially, or sexually?
   • How did this person affect my goals physically, emotionally, spiritually, mentally, socially, educationally, culturally, financially, or sexually?

5. Once you finish the "How I Was Affected" column, look for the patterns. Is there a pattern? Are you angry with a lot of people? In the above examples, the writer might see how difficult it has been for him to take an action in supporting his beliefs. He may need a lot of support in growing through his inventory. He can look at why. He may need some group support to mirror back to him how he is realistically viewed, instead of only how his father viewed him. As patterns are revealed, ask yourself, "How am I contributing to this pattern? What can I do to change how I am in the world?" For some people, this is very intense and frightening. You may want to have someone to share your experiences with. Write what you discover in "How I Can Change This Pattern" column.

- If you can, discuss your list with an elder, mentor, spiritual advisor, or trusted friend. Ask for help in figuring out what you can do to meet your needs first and then what you can reasonably expect from others.

- Begin to adjust your expectations and behavior. Begin to use time and energy to develop the skills and abilities that will lead to you feeling fulfilled, content, and confident. For example, if you have a history of letting yourself be used, learn how to say "no." Read books on the subject, take assertiveness training, go to counseling, or join groups where you can practice new behaviors in safety.

How I Was Affected	How I Can Change This Pattern
I was heartbroken to lose my dog. He meant everything to me. I didn't get another pet until I was an adult. This affected me spiritually and emotionally.	I can write a letter to my pet and say the good-bye I never got to tell him. Maybe then I won't be so nervous about caring.
I feel scared that my uncle may not get well. I am being affected emotionally, spiritually, and socially.	I can talk with my uncle and then contact my congressional representative, as well as see whether there is a group working toward more benefits for veterans.
I feel terribly sad that I couldn't get through to my father. This affected my sense of emotional safety. It	I need to get some counseling to help me let go of what happened. My father is dead, but his ideas live on in me

affected me spiritually, emotionally, socially, and maybe financially because I don't think much of myself.	and they are holding me back. I need some help.

CONCLUSION

Emotional inventories suggest ways of resurrecting layers of old unresolved emotions. We can do them slowly or quickly, but as we do them, we can expect to feel or re-experience these emotions, sometimes in bursts. Exercise common sense. For example, if you tend to act out when angry, don't try tackling a lot of people on your list at one time. Pace yourself and ask for help.

Recommended Reading

Bradshaw, John. *Healing the Shame That Binds You.* Deerfield Beach, Fla.: Health Communications, 1988. This book details family systems. Intergenerational histories, built on discipline through shaming, result in creating family failures over time.

Claremont de Castillejo, Irene. *Knowing Woman: A Feminine Psychology.* Boston: Shambhala, 1997. This book explores, through Jungian ideas, the various aspects of our personalities, including shadow aspects, feminine aspects, and masculine aspects. The author's examples are extremely clear and useful.

Evans, Patricia. *The Verbally Abusive Relationship: How to Recognize It and How to Respond.* 2d ed. Holbrook, Mass.: Adams Media Corporation, 1996. This book offers very pointed information about what delimits abusers and those who become part of their system. Evans points out succinctly how any interaction may be viewed through the abuser's eyes and the survivor's eyes. She explains well how the vulnerabilities in one are so helpful for getting the other what he or she wants.

———. *Verbal Abuse Survivors Speak Out on Relationships and Recovery.* Holbrook, Mass.: Adams Media Corporation, 1993. Survivors and perpetrators reveal various aspects of the abuse/victim cycle through personal stories. Their experiences highlight what interventions effectively stop the cycle.

Harris, Bud. *Sacred Selfishness: A Guide to Living a Life of Substance.* Makawao, Hawaii: Inner Ocean Publishing, Inc., 2002. Harris offers many fine suggestions to help adults through developmental challenges. The success stories ring true, and his use of Jungian methods is pragmatic and accessible.

Hillman, James. *The Soul's Code: In Search of Character and Calling.* New York: Warner Books, Inc., 1996. This book looks at the core interior journey and validates the process of seeking those challenges that satisfy the "DNA" of one's basic identity.

Levoy, Gregg. *Callings: Finding and Following an Authentic Life.* New York: Three Rivers Press, 1997. Levoy's book functions as a good mentor might: sharing information and wisdom along with plenty of room for thinking things over. It is a friendly look at what we may be "called" to do.

Rando, Therese A. *Treatment of Complicated Mourning.* Champaign, Ill.: Research Press, 1993. This book covers all aspects of loss, and it ties in physical and emotional problems with unresolved loss. The inventory and questionnaire at the back are excellent guides for considering when loss has not been worked through.

Wegscheider-Cruse, Sharon. *Another Chance: Hope and Health for the Alcoholic Family.* 2d ed. Palo Alto, Calif.: Science and Behavior Books, 1989. This is the best book I have read on family systems, birth order, and roles that must be played out for the survival of the family as a system.

Index

About the Author

As a social worker and therapist, Erika Hunter found that many colleagues and clients, through no fault of their own, were limited in using their emotional lives as powerful agents for change. She also found that the abused children, poverty-stricken families, and chemically dependent clients she worked with lacked an emotional vocabulary. The result is this book, which outlines emotional responsibility, social accountability, and the use of everyday interactions to create solutions, healing, and understanding. Hunter lives in New England.

Hazelden Publishing and Educational Services is a division of the Hazelden Foundation, a not-for-profit organization. Since 1949, Hazelden has been a leader in promoting the dignity and treatment of people afflicted with the disease of chemical dependency.

The mission of the foundation is to improve the quality of life for individuals, families, and communities by providing a national continuum of information, education, and recovery services that are widely accessible; to advance the field through research and training; and to improve our quality and effectiveness through continuous improvement and innovation.

Stemming from that, the mission of this division is to provide quality information and support to people wherever they may be in their personal journey—from education and early intervention, through treatment and recovery, to personal and spiritual growth.

Although our treatment programs do not necessarily use everything Hazelden publishes, our bibliotherapeutic materials support our mission and the Twelve Step philosophy upon which it is based. We encourage your comments and feedback.

The headquarters of the Hazelden Foundation are in Center City, Minnesota. Additional treatment facilities are located in Chicago, Illinois; Newberg, Oregon; New York, New York; Plymouth, Minnesota; St. Paul, Minnesota; and West Palm Beach, Florida. At these sites, we provide a continuum of care for men and women of all ages. Our Plymouth facility is designed specifically for youth and families.

For more information on Hazelden, please call **1-800-257-7800.** Or you may access our World Wide Web site on the Internet at **www.hazelden.org.**